MASSACHUSETTS
Off the Beaten Path

D1466796

MASSACHUSETTS
Off the Beaten Path™

by Patricia Mandell

A Voyager Book

The
Globe
Pequot
Press

Chester, Connecticut

The prices and rates listed in this guidebook were confirmed at press time. We recommend, however, that you call establishments before traveling to obtain current information.

Copyright © 1992 by Patricia Mandell

Cover and text illustrations by Carole Drong

Library of Congress Cataloging-in-Publication Data

Mandell, Patricia.

   Massachusetts, off the beaten path / by Patricia Mandell. —
   1st ed.
      p.   cm.
   "A Voyager book."
   Includes index.
   ISBN 0-87106-242-9
   1. Massachusetts—Description and travel—1981- —Guidebooks. I. Title
   F62.3.M35 1992
   917.4404'43—dc 20   91-25494
                                                CIP

Manufactured in the United States of America
First Edition/First Printing

Contents

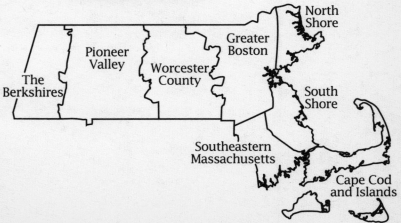

MASSACHUSETTS

To Eliot and Allie,
who were so much
a part of the journey

Introduction

Almost the entire state of Massachusetts is off the beaten path, quietly waiting to be discovered. Yes, Boston and Cape Cod and its island neighbors must batten their hatches against the invasion of summer visitors. Likewise, Tanglewood in the Berkshires. And yes, Massachusetts is New England's most populous state and its most densely settled one.

But even in downtown Boston, New England's largest city, there are little-known places where the tourists don't go. Admire the artworks in the galleries of the Leather District—Boston's Soho. Find out why you should visit Boston's tiny Chinatown. Walk the nation's first Women's Heritage Trail, or visit Castle Island, where Edgar Allan Poe conceived "The Cask of Amontillado."

And Boston is just the beginning of the journey. This book covers eight regions, from the Cape to the Berkshires, highlighting almost 200 attractions in detail. The choices were often arbitrary, because there are actually hundreds more. But making those choices was a lot of fun; you never can tell when straying from the well-beaten path will lead you to a llama farm, or a small-town library basement full of pre-Columbian pottery. In truth, this book barely scratches the surface of the off-the-beaten-path possibilities in this state. Think of it as a taste of some of the best.

Massachusetts's best includes unique scenic wonders, from glacial potholes big enough to swim in to a "natural" bridge that nature made out of marble. You can spend the night in a lighthouse on a windswept island off the coast of Cape Cod or visit a reservation where sixty-five varieties of holly grow.

This book will help you discover such man-made wonders as the Bridge of Flowers, a millionaires' row rivaling Newport's, and the longest wooden bridge on the East Coast. American history has its deepest roots in Massachusetts. You'll visit the homes of John Adams, Daniel Webster, and John Alden. But you'll also meet some distinctly lesser-known historic personages, such as "the witch of Wall Street" and "the Copper King."

You will tour museums devoted to everything from the legendary Tom Thumb to dolls, shipbuilding, and Shakers. At farms and orchards, you'll sample Massachusetts's largesse: chèvres, maple syrup, cider, and cranberry wine, to name just a few.

Revel in the quirky place and the oddball attraction too: a house made entirely of newsprint, the country's only vintage plumbing museum, a giant milk bottle serving as an ice-cream stand.

Massachusetts is where you'll find the country's oldest continuously operating museum and its oldest continuously operating church, the oldest art festival, and the longest-running carillon concert series in North America.

This state's beaches and parks are some of its most special places. Take the hidden barrier beach on Nantucket, reachable only by four-wheel drive. Or the North Shore park that was once a wealthy family's estate and still has its carriage trails and rhododendrons and laurels.

Some of Massachusetts's best-kept secrets are off-season delights, such as wintertime cruises to see harbor seals. Even the shops are an adventure. One sells shining antique potbellied stoves; another is an eighteenth-century wooden boat shop.

When you're hungry, stop in at a country restaurant serving seventeen kinds of pie, a nineteenth-century ice-cream parlor that still makes egg creams, or a mom-and-pop eatery where you can get fish cakes and baked beans at breakfast. There's also a tearoom serving scones and cream, as well as a romantic alfresco dessert-only spot overlooking a salt marsh on the Cape.

Bed-and-breakfast inns along the way offer a comfortable and friendly place to lay your head at night during your travels. Say hello for me.

For their generous help in researching this book, I would like to thank Ashley McCown of the Massachusetts Office of Travel and Tourism, Brooks Kelly of the Plymouth County Development Council, Sheila Pina of the Bristol County Development Council, Anjeljean Chiaramida of the Martha's Vineyard Chamber of Commerce, Libby Oldham of the Nantucket Island Chamber of Commerce, Milly Spence of the Worcester Convention and Visitors Bureau, Ann Hamilton of the Franklin County Chamber of Commerce, and Judy Salsbury of the Berkshires Visitors Bureau. Last but not least, thanks to Patty Picco, who made it possible.

Off the Beaten Path in Greater Boston

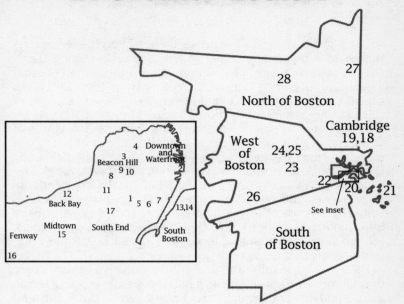

1. Historic Neighborhoods Foundation
2. Seal pool
3. Harrison Gray Otis House
4. Commonwealth Brewing Co.
5. Chinatown
6. Leather District
7. South Station
8. Acorn Street
9. Hidden Gardens of Beacon Hill
10. State House
11. Swan Boats
12. Gibson House
13. Children's Museum
14. Computer Museum
15. Mapparium

16. Isabella Stewart Gardner Museum
17. Bay Village
18. Harvard University's museums
19. Mt. Auburn Cemetery
20. Castle Island
21. Boston Harbor Islands
22. Frederick Law Olmsted National Historic Site
23. Gore Place
24. DeCordova Museum
25. Gropius House
26. Garden in the Woods
27. Bay Circuit Trail
28. New England Quilt Museum

Greater Boston

On any given day in downtown Boston, you'll see tourists rooted to a painted red line on the sidewalk, staring trans-fixedly at their maps. The ribbon of red marks the Freedom Trail, and they are happy to follow it to the Old North Church, Faneuil Hall, and Paul Revere's House—in and out of town in one day. But they miss 95 percent of what's here.

Step off the Freedom Trail and you'll discover a world of neighborhoods so distinct that traveling among them is like traveling from village to village—which these neighborhoods once were. You would never mistake the brownstones and wide Parisian boulevards of the Back Bay for the brick Federal-style houses and narrow nineteenth-century lanes of Beacon Hill. The old waterfront wharf buildings have been remade into condos and shops, dwarfed by towering luxury hotels. Rather than clipper ships, today it is cruise boats and commuter boats that depart the quays.

The industrial landscape of South Boston also houses some unique museums and the city's fish piers and shipping termi-nals. Though almost no tourist knows where the South End is, it's the city's largest neighborhood. It, like the Back Bay, was built on filled-in land but long before the Back Bay was. The South End's Victorian brick townhouses bear a striking similarity to those of Back Bay. Despite the scruffy character of the Fenway, which winds around the Back Bay Fens, it too holds hidden treasure. The Midtown area wears a 1960s urban-renewal look but holds such nineteenth-century archi-tectural masterpieces as Trinity Church and the Boston Pub-lic Library. The size of Boston's Chinatown doesn't rival New York's or San Francisco's, but its heart does. The more far-flung areas of Cambridge and towns to the west and north are not to be overlooked either.

Boston is a compact and walkable city—just don't try to drive here. For complete travel information, contact the Greater Boston Convention and Visitors Bureau, Prudential Plaza West, P.O. Box 490, Boston 02199; (617) 536–4100.

Downtown and Waterfront

The best way to get to know Boston's neighborhoods is by taking a tour with the **Historic Neighborhoods Foundation.** HNF focuses on one neighborhood at a time. In summer, weekly tours visit the waterfront and Chinatown. Tours of the Italian North End go off the Freedom Trail to find hidden courtyards and gardens and to discover its social history. Special semiannual programs center on the interiors of Back Bay and Beacon Hill townhouses, the Victorian-era homes of Dorchester, and the streetcar suburbs of Roslindale and Roxbury. Write HNF at 2 Boylston Street, Boston, 02116, or call (617) 426–1885. Tours cost $5.00 per person.

You can amuse yourself endlessly outside the New England Aquarium on Central Wharf (617–973–5200) as well as inside. Outside is where you'll find the **seal pool,** where a half-dozen harbor seals cavort endlessly behind a glass wall so that you can see them. With their big brown eyes that look almost human, smiley mouths, and fans of stiff white whiskers, the seals are irresistible. The star of the show is Rigel. Prompted with a tasty bit of herring, Rigel says "Hi" in a gruffly guttural tone. His trainers hope to expand his vocabulary. You can watch the training sessions at unscheduled times in the morning, afternoon, and evening.

While they stroll the waterfront, many people don't look beyond the shops and offices. But a plaque here and there will tell you how much history is here. Look at the facades and you'll see that some of the old warehouses were designed to emulate Renaissance palazzos and Greek temples. John Hancock had his countinghouse on cobblestoned Long Wharf. Built in 1760, the countinghouse is now the Chart House restaurant and still has Hancock's black iron safe embedded in the wall. Nathaniel Hawthorne served as a customs inspector at Long Wharf. Built in 1710, Long Wharf is the granddaddy of all the wharves. The British marched ashore on Long Wharf when they occupied the city in 1768, and they beat a hasty retreat back down it when the colonists routed them out in 1776. In later years, Long Wharf bid adieu to missionaries, California Gold Rush hopefuls, and clipper traders. One little jewel you should look for is Waterfront Park (immediately north of Long Wharf on Atlantic Avenue), a nicely landscaped pocket park with brick walkways and benches that offers a lovely harbor view along with respite.

Four centuries of notable Boston women's tales have been collected along the Women's Heritage Trail, believed to be the country's first. Four walking routes cover downtown, the North End, Beacon Hill, and the South Cove/Chinatown area, linking the stories of some fifty women. Among them are Phillis Wheatley, a slave who became the first African-American woman poet, and Abigail Adams, wife of President John Adams. Louisa May Alcott lived on Beacon Hill, and Fannie Merritt Farmer published her world-famous cookbook from Tremont Street. Walks are given periodically for a small donation. Self-guided maps are available at the Boston Common Visitor Information kiosk on Tremont Street and at the National Park Service Visitor Information, at 15 State Street (617–242–5642). For more information, write the Women's Heritage Trail, P.O. Box 833, Boston 02120, or call (617) 541–9054.

Steps away from Government Center, the **Harrison Gray Otis House** conceals behind its Federal exterior one of the most opulent interiors in Boston. This three-story brick house, built in 1796, was the first of three that Charles Bulfinch designed for his friend Otis, a prominent lawyer and member of Congress. Everywhere you look are imported wallpapers and carpets, heavy swag curtains, and gilt-framed mirrors. High-relief dancing figures of maidens grace an Adams-style mantel in the drawing room. Neoclassical motifs frame every doorway and window; a ceiling border depicts scenes of Pompeii. The house, at 141 Cambridge Street, is headquarters for the Society for the Preservation of New England Antiquities (617–227–3956). It's open from noon to 5:00 P.M. Tuesday through Friday and from 10:00 A.M. to 5:00 P.M. Saturday. Admission is $3.00 for adults and $1.50 for children.

Right next to the Harrison Gray Otis House, at 131 Cambridge Street, is the Old West Church, designed by an architect as famous as Charles Bulfinch: Asher Benjamin. Benjamin wrote handbooks for builders and carpenters to guide them in working with his neoclassical style, influencing American architecture from the East Coast to the Midwest. Designed in 1805, Old West is a signature model of simplicity and symmetry. Three brick stories narrow to an Ionic cupola and a

Doric third-story porch, with the gables of each story topped by graceful urns. The cupola has twelve columns flanking a clock garlanded in the Adamesque style.

A few blocks from Cambridge Street is a restaurant that will delight beer fans: the **Commonwealth Brewing Co.,** at 138 Portland Street (617–523–8383), which makes all its own beer in the basement. There are more than a dozen varieties on tap, plus several seasonal brews, such as a cinnamon-and-orange-scented spiced ale. Copper and brass shine everywhere in the vast dining room, where enormous beer kegs stand about. Dinners range from grilled fresh fish and prime rib to meat pie and three-alarm chili. Downstairs in the taproom you can watch the English-trained brewers at work behind glass walls while you sit in a Hofbrau-style bar.

Although few people think to walk inside the New England Telephone building, at 185 Franklin Street, inside it is one of the most splendid murals in town. Called *Telephone Men and Women at Work,* it circles the rotunda in a 197-foot oval, 12 feet high. The mural shows telephone history, starting with a muttonchopped Alexander Graham Bell giving a telephone demonstration in Salem in 1877. Scenes of the 1880s are rich in period detail of top-hatted gents and long-gowned women. Also in the building is Alexander Graham Bell's Garret, a dark little corner full of memorabilia where Bell worked to develop the telephone in 1875.

Except for its restaurants, most guidebooks never bother to list Boston's tiny **Chinatown.** Chinatown may be small, but it's intensely and authentically Chinese. Green-pagoda-topped gates guarded by Chinese Foo dogs mark the entrance, at the intersection of Beach Street and Surface Road. Even the phone booths are covered with red and green Chinese pagodas. Stores and restaurants advertise in Chinese characters. Among the shops you might poke into are Eastern Live Poultry, at 48 Beach Street (617–426–5960), which sells squawking live chickens; Hing Shing Pastry, at 67 Beach Street (617–451–1162), for its mouth-watering array of traditional Chinese pastries; and Chin Enterprises, Inc., at 33 Harrison Avenue (617–423–1725), where you can buy a professional-quality wok. Restaurants fill every block, but one of the more intriguing ones is the Chinatown Eatery, at 44 Beach Street, which resembles a Hong Kong food market in its bedlam. Five take-out stands surround cafeteria-style tables, and menus on the wall are handwritten in Chinese as well as English.

At the corner of Harrison Avenue and Oak Street, you'll see a building-size mural that depicts the history of the Chinese in Boston—the *Unity/Community Chinatown Mural.* Among its pigtailed Chinese figures are construction workers, a launderer, and women at sewing machines.

For a window on Chinese culture, stop in at the Chinese-Culture Institute at 272 Tremont Street (617–542–4599), which exhibits the work of Chinese artists. Other offerings include concerts, plays, and workshops in traditional crafts. The annual Chinese Lantern Festival celebrating the Chinese New Year sets the streets to glowing with lanterns and features a splendid costumed parade.

Another little-known Boston enclave is the **Leather District,** right next door to Chinatown, bounded by Kneeland Street and Atlantic Avenue. Once the heart of New England's shoe industry, this area has been reborn as Boston's Soho. Art galleries now inhabit South Street's grand old Richardsonian buildings. These are serious galleries, and they hang some really cutting-edge stuff.

Going up South Street, you'll see local artists' avant-garde creations at the Bromfield Gallery (No. 90) and contemporary abstract art at Kimball Bourgault (No. 100). Abstract paintings hang at the Howard Yezerski Gallery (No. 186) and fine art photographs at the Robert Klein Gallery (No. 207). Several other galleries are in the same building at 207 South Street: Thomas Segal, Mario Diacono, and the Akin Gallery. Yet more galleries are the Nicole C. Gallery, at 745 Atlantic Avenue; and the JMW Gallery, at 144 Lincoln Street, which deals in Arts & Crafts furniture and pottery. Exhibits rotate monthly, and the visitor can happen into a wine-and-cheese opening reception to meet the artist.

Of the handful of restaurants, one that blends superbly into these artistic quarters is the Loading Zone, at 150 Kneeland Street (617–695–0087). Behind gray garage doors, the dining room showcases artists' creations in glass shadowboxes that serve as tabletops. In their works the artists used everything from collage, found objects, and trash to holograms, video, and sound. The food isn't bad either: barbecued meats and seafood.

Almost next door, the Blue Diner, at 178 Kneeland Street (617–338–4639), is a real diner right in the middle of Boston, sparkling with blue neon and chrome, plus jukebox. There are lines out the door here, and so it's best to come in the off-hours for a snack, late lunch, or breakfast.

You might also consider lunching at nearby **South Station,** whose curved, 1898 beaux arts facade fronts on Summer Street and Atlantic Avenue. Once terribly dilapidated, South Station has been gorgeously restored, its interior designed to resemble a European market square. The light-filled concourse sparkles with polished marble floors, brass railings, gleaming oak benches, and restaurants and shops under elegant dark green kiosks. This is now such a wonderful place to just be that Bostonians actually come here for lunch or coffee, as well as summer jazz concerts. On sale are flowers, gourmet chocolates, foreign magazines, freshly baked croissants, frozen yogurt, and perfume.

If you're looking for an off-the-beaten-path place to stay in Boston, you could try one of the bed-and-breakfast services. They might place you in a brick Federal home on Beacon Hill with fireplaces, four-posters, and a lovely hidden garden; a classic 1890 Back Bay brownstone with mahogany floors; or perhaps a South End Victorian townhouse. Here are three services: Bed & Breakfast Associates Bay Colony (Box 57–166 Babson Park, Boston 02157–0166; 800–347–5088 or 617–449–5302; doubles $65–$100), A Bed & Breakfast above the Rest (50 Boatswain's Way, Suite 105, Boston 02150; 617–884–7748, 617–277–2292, or 800–677–2262 outside Massachusetts), and Bed & Breakfast Agency of Boston (47 Commercial Wharf, Boston 02110; 617–720–3540 or 800–248–9262; doubles $70–$110), which specializes in the downtown area. Some services also have accommodations in Cambridge or farther afield.

Beacon Hill and Back Bay

One of the most photographed streets on Beacon Hill is tiny **Acorn Street,** a nineteenth-century byway only one lane wide and one block long. The antique charm of this street is undiminished. Acorn Street is so remarkably unchanged that it's easy to picture a horse and carriage rumbling down it. It's one of the few old cobblestoned streets left on Beacon Hill and one,of the oldest-looking places in Boston. Coachmen and servants of the wealthy once lived on Acorn Street. Their Federal brick townhouses resembled their employers' mansions, graced with black shutters and windowboxes, as well as black iron gaslights. Acorn Street is 1 block north of Chestnut Street, between West Cedar and Willow streets.

Behind Beacon Hill houses are lovely, walled hidden gardens. Some are opened to the public during the **Hidden Gardens of Beacon Hill** tour the third Thursday in May. The tour reveals how artfully these tiny backyard spaces have been landscaped, with everything from flowering shrubs to herbs and some very old trees. Unusual accents might be a Japanese wind sculpture, stone Cupids, antique French urns, or painted faux trellises. For tickets, which include refreshments, write the Beacon Hill Garden Club, Box 302, Charles Street Station, Boston 02114, or call (617) 227–4392. Tickets cost $12 in advance and $15 on tour day.

Charles Bulfinch won his fame for designing the Massachusetts **State House.** Its regal facade crowns the summit of Beacon Hill. Freedom Trail tourists dutifully regard the outside but don't bother with the inside. Yet inside, you'll see a patterned floor made of twenty-four kinds of marble, murals of the American Revolution, and hundreds of historic flags returned after duty in American wars. A stained-glass skylight depicts the seals of the original thirteen colonies. The black iron railings leading up the elegantly wide main staircase are a unique pattern of grillwork called "black lace"; the molds were broken after the railings were cast. Don't miss the Sacred Cod in the House of Representatives—a wooden fish hung there in 1784 to symbolize the importance of the fishing industry to Massachusetts. Free tours are given from 10:00 A.M. to 4:00 P.M. weekdays. Call (617) 727–3676.

Hidden away a half-block behind the State House is a great find in an inexpensive restaurant, called Tangiers, at 37 Bowdoin Street (617–367–0273). A bistro-style basement cafe, Tangiers specializes in such home-cooked Middle Eastern foods as stuffed grape leaves, Middle Eastern pizza, and chicken or lamb kebabs, as well as more than ninety Middle

Swan Boats, Boston Public Garden

Eastern drinks and an assortment of Middle Eastern dessert pastries.

Down on Charles Street is a comfortable coffeehouse where you can linger luxuriously in the European manner over espresso or cappuccino. Il Dolce Momento, at 30 Charles Street (617–720–0477), also serves hearty Italian sandwiches and homemade soups. Specialties are fresh *gelato* made in-house, croissants, and flaky Italian pastries.

One of the most enduring symbols of Boston are the famous **Swan Boats** that sail the lagoon in the Public Garden. The Swan Boats were launched in 1877 by Robert Paget, who was inspired by the swan-boat scene in Wagner's opera *Lohengrin.* They have been operated by the Paget family ever since. Many Bostonians never ride these boats; I did not for ten years. The big surprise is that riding the Swan Boats is still fun. These unique boats make a leisurely circuit of the lagoon, trailed by quacking ducks certain of a handout. The Swan Boats operate from mid-April to mid-September; tickets cost $1.25 for adults and 75 cents for children. Call (617) 522–1966.

With all the homage paid to colonial and Federal architecture in Boston, the Victorian age gets short shrift. But at the **Gibson House,** a Victorian house museum, you can see the life-style of the Back Bay Victorians in all its full-blown opulence. This Italian Renaissance Revival home maintains its original 1859 interior of gold-embossed faux leather wallpaper and black walnut paneling. Family pieces include plush Turkish ottomans, eighteenth-century heirloom furniture, china and porcelain, and paintings and photographs. The Gibson House, at 137 Beacon Street, is open from Wednesday through Sunday, May through October, and weekends in winter. Tours are given at 1:00, 2:00, and 3:00 P.M. Admission is $3.00. Call (617) 267–6338.

If you're a Francophile, check out the French Library, a unique bastion of French culture in an 1867 Back Bay townhouse, located at 53 Marlborough Street (617–266–4351). The library was founded after World War II by a group of Free French enthusiasts. French films and concerts are held in the exquisite Louis XV theater, with its carved French paneling accented in gold leaf. Films range from old Jean Luc Godard and Marcel Carne classics on up to contemporary. A candlelight concert series presents French music, plus wine and cheese; art shows, cooking demonstrations, and lectures are also offered. The highlight of the year is Bastille Day (July 14), celebrated with a bang-up dinner and block dance.

South Boston

South Boston is home to two unique museums. When you cross the Congress Street Bridge, you'll see a giant white milk bottle, the Hood Milk Bottle. A lunch stand in the 1930s, it sells snacks today and signals the beginning of Museum Wharf.

If you have children, you won't want to miss the **Children's Museum,** one of the best in the country. It's also the country's second oldest, founded in 1913. There are four floors of hands-on exhibits here, many creative and witty. A skeleton wearing a top hat and bow tie illustrates anatomy. Children can blow bubbles at the giant bubblemaker, or clamber up a two-story climbing sculpture of chicken wire and wood. A mock garage and a neighborhood market teach children about jobs. An exhibit on multiculturism, racism, and ethnicity, to prepare children for a multicultural nation, is the first of its kind in the country. The museum is at 300 Congress Street (617–426–6500). Admission is $6.00 for adults, $5.00 for children ages two to fifteen, and $2.00 for one-year-olds. From September to June, the museum is open from 10:00 A.M. to 5:00 P.M. Tuesday through Sunday and until 9:00 P.M. Friday; Friday evenings, admission is only $1.00 per person. From July through Labor Day, the museum also opens Mondays.

Upstairs in the same brick building is the world's only museum devoted solely to computers—the **Computer Museum.** Just how fast technology changes is dramatically illustrated in the exhibits, which cover more than forty years of computing. Whereas an early U.S. Air Force vacuum-tube computer took up the space of a four-story building, the same computing power is now available in a desktop microcomputer. You can see the CAD/CAM program used to design the sole of a Nike Air shoe; you can also see "smart" robots, animated films, and a computer made of 10,000 Tinker Toys that actually works. You might design a car on-screen, or have Aaron the computer artist draw your picture. To really see how computers work, take a stroll through the giant Walk-through Computer, with its 25-foot keyboard and bumper-car-size mouse. The Computer Museum keeps the same hours as the Children's Museum. Admission is $6.00 for adults, $5.00 for students, and half-price Saturday mornings until noon. Call (617) 426–2800.

South Boston is a peninsula lined with commercial fishing and shipping piers, a spot most tourists don't investigate unless there's a big exhibition on at the World Trade Center or unless they're intending to dine at Anthony's Pier Four or Jimmy's Harborside. But the Fish Piers, right near Jimmy's on Northern Avenue, are a lively scene at dawn, when the fishing boats return to port to unload their catch. The fresh catch is sold at auction right off the boats. You can see rubber-booted workers clean the fish in wooden sheds.

Midtown, Fenway, South End

When you're traveling, you might not think to stop at the library. But the Boston Public Library is worth a visit even if you never check out a book. The library has so many artistic and architectural creations that tours of them are given regularly. It was built in 1895 in Copley Square, after the manner of an Italian Renaissance palace. Daniel Chester French did the elegant relief work on the massive bronze doors. The grand entrance hall (now entered via a side door) sweeps up an imposing marble staircase past twin stone lions. The sienna-colored marble also forms arches and Corinthian columns that frame frescoes of the muses. The landing overlooks a lovely central courtyard with a fountain and benches. A second-floor room, based on the library of the Venetian Doge's Palace, is dominated by a mural of the Holy Grail painted by Edwin Austin Abbey. Murals by John Singer Sargent, paintings by John Singleton Copley, and sculptures by Augustus and Louis Saint-Gaudens also grace the library. The library's main entrance is at 666 Boylston Street; call (617) 536–5400, ext. 212.

The world's only stained-glass globe big enough to walk through is located at the First Church of Christ, Scientist. Thirty feet in diameter, the **Mapparium** represented the "global village" long before that concept was popular. Six hundred and eight glass panels make up the countries of 1931, sending visitors' voices echoing hollowly. A glass bridge spans the middle, where you can get a bird's-eye view of any country in the world—the architect's intention. Although onlookers once could see through the bridge beneath their feet to Antarctica, it so much bothered people to be standing in the middle of nowhere that the church put a carpet down. The Mapparium, at 175 Huntington Avenue, is open Monday through Saturday from 9:30 A.M. to 4:00 P.M. Call (617) 450–2000.

Although a 1990 multimillion-dollar art heist focused international attention on the **Isabella Stewart Gardner Museum,** it still gets bypassed in favor of the Museum of Fine Arts. Hidden away behind a deceptively unprepossessing exterior is a fifteenth-century-style Venetian palazzo. Enter through a four-story courtyard with stone porticoes, arches, and columns; beautiful flowering plants; and Moorish-style windows. It's a suitably fabulous showcase for the personal art collection of Mrs. Isabella Stewart Gardner, a wealthy Victorian matron whose independent spirit provoked Bostonians to label her an eccentric. "Mrs. Jack" liked to wear her two largest diamonds on gold wire springs over her head, among other unusual habits. Her collection, amassed over a lifetime of travel to Europe and opened in 1903, spans an extraordinary range: Roman sarcophagi, Chinese porcelain, Flemish tapestries, Italian Renaissance paintings, American and British paintings, sculpture, furniture, and many prints and drawings. The museum also has a lunchtime cafe and offers weekly chamber music concerts and Thursday-afternoon tours. It's located at 280 The Fenway; call (617) 566-1401. Tickets cost $6.00. The museum is open from noon to 5:00 P.M. Tuesday through Sunday (till 6:30 on Tuesdays).

Boston's largest neighborhood, the South End, is listed on the National Register of Historic Places as the largest concentration of Victorian brick row houses in the country. Once the height of fashionable living, it was eclipsed by the Back Bay and lapsed into decline. But in the 1960s, an influx of professionals renovated the dilapidated buildings. They drew chic boutiques, restaurants, and nightclubs in their wake, which line the main thoroughfares of Columbus Avenue and Tremont Street. The neighborhood has a Bohemian edge, lent by the many artists and gays living here. South End artists exhibit regularly at the Mills Gallery, at 549 Tremont Street (617–426–7700). In late October, annual house tours are given by the South End Historical Society, at 532 Massachusetts Avenue (617–536–4445). The jewel of the South End is **Bay Village,** the few blocks just southeast of Arlington and Stuart streets. This warren of narrow streets looks more like Beacon Hill than Back Bay. Black shutters and iron grillwork doorways and windowboxes accent its brick row houses. And wrought-iron gaslights stand on the sidewalks, just as they do on Beacon Hill.

Cambridge

Not nearly so famous as Boston's museums, **Harvard University's museums** are real treasures. From ancient Chinese jades to dinosaur bones, these museums have it all. The University Museum is four museums in one, housing exhibits on botany, gems and minerals, zoology, and archaeology and ethnology. The spirit of nineteenth-century collectors, who chased through jungles and mountains with their butterfly nets and specimen boxes, lingers here in the antique, glass-topped wooden display cases. The Botanical Museum's most celebrated exhibit is the Glass Flowers, handmade glass replicas of 847 species of plants for teaching botany. The first time I saw them, I walked by them, thinking, "Oh, those are real," and looking elsewhere for the glass flowers. Strawberry and peach blossoms, wood rush, and palm leaves made of colored glass and wire rest gently in their cases; larger-than-life glass bees pollinate some specimens. In the Peabody Museum of Archaeology and Ethnology, prehistoric and historic cultures from pre-Columbian Central American peoples to South American and North American Indians highlight the collections. Whale skeletons hang on the ceiling of the Museum of Comparative Zoology, where rooms full of stuffed beasties include everything from butterflies, beetles, and fish to a Mongolian tiger and 600 species of hummingbirds. The Mineralogical and Geological Museums collection was begun in 1784 and ranges from precious gems to meteorites. The University Museum, at 24 Oxford Street, is open from 9:00 A.M. to 4:30 P.M. Monday through Saturday and from 1:00 P.M. Sunday. Admission is $3.00 for aduts and $1.00 for children (for all four museums). Call (617) 495–3045.

Harvard has three art museums, all close together. The Busch-Reisinger Museum, at 24 Kirkland Street, with its important collections of Central and Northern European art, is the only such museum in the country. The Fogg Art Museum, at 32 Quincy Street, holds master paintings by Fra Angelico, Rubens, van Gogh, Renoir, Homer, and Pollock. In a strikingly contemporary building opened in 1985, the Sackler Museum, at 485 Broadway, displays ancient, Near Eastern, and Oriental art, including an unparalleled collection of Chinese jades and cave reliefs. The art museums are open Tuesday through Sunday from 10:00 A.M. to 5:00 P.M. Admission is $4.00 for adults; children under eighteen are admitted free. Call (617) 495–9400 for information.

If you have traveled the subway systems of Paris and Stockholm, their artwork may have impressed you. Cambridge has this country's first and largest such program, called Arts on the Line. Stations on the Red Line and the Orange Line showcase dozens of works of art. These are always a lift to see when you're riding the subway. Besides a bright red windmill sculpture, there's a shimmering mobile made of aluminum and Mylar planes. Other works include a whimsical mural of black-and-white cows and a life-size statue group of a young family of four. Lost gloves immortalized in bronze along an escalator railing draw people to touch them as they ride.

Especially in the spring, there's no more beautiful place in Cambridge to be than **Mt. Auburn Cemetery.** Acres of flowering plants and trees surround the graves in America's first garden cemetery, founded in 1831. Everywhere you look, trees towering over your head hang their soft petals of pink, white, lavender, and yellow over the graves, gently obscuring the rough stone. A weeping willow leans soulfully into a pond. Many of the 2,500 trees in 380 species are rare, such as cedar of Lebanon, weeping flowering dogwood, and White Russian mulberry. But no less beautiful are the more common varieties: star magnolia, Corinthian dogwoods, several varieties of cherry trees, and purple crabapple. The trees attract so many birds that birders come here to see them, and the cemetery is one of the best places to see the spring warbler migration. Other birds bring the number of species sighted in Mt. Auburn to more than 235. And most of those famous Bostonians whose names you recognize are buried here—Henry Wadsworth Longfellow, Winslow Homer, Oliver Wendell Holmes, Charles Bulfinch, Amy Lowell, Julia Ward Howe, Henry Cabot Lodge, R. Buckminster Fuller, and Isabella Stewart Gardner, to name just a few. A map of the graves is available at the gate house. Burials take place every day, and you cannot picnic, jog, play Frisbee, or otherwise disport yourself in a disrespectful manner. The main cemetery gates are at 580 Mt. Auburn Street (Route 16). The Friends of Mt. Auburn Cemetery (617–864–9646) leads seasonal walks and gives lectures on the cemetery year-round.

One of the few bed-and-breakfasts that you can book independently in Cambridge is called A Cambridge House, an 1892 home listed on the National Register of Historic Places. It's nicely restored and richly furnished with floral print fabrics, patterned wallpapers, period antiques, and Oriental rugs. A number of rooms are located in the adjacent Carriage House and in another nearby property. Write A Cambridge

House at 2218 Massachusetts Avenue, Cambridge 02140, or call (617) 491–6300 (doubles $105–$175).

South of Boston

Even before you get to Boston, there's an unusual sight on Route 3. Heading north, look to your right at exit 13 and you'll see two white Boston Gas Company tanks. One of them is painted with huge swashes of bright colors in a rainbow of red, yellow, orange, blue, green, and purple. The rainbow gives life to a dreary urban landscape. It's signed simply "Corita." The artist was the late Corita Kent, a former Los Angeles nun who resigned her order and moved to Boston. She designed the popular "LOVE" postage stamp and countless pop art silk-screen prints. Her design has been a Boston landmark ever since 1971 and is the world's largest copyrighted work of art. During the Vietnam War, many criticized the design, saying the blue stripe resembled the profile of North Vietnamese leader Ho Chi Minh. Corita denied it. Since a second tank is no longer needed, the rainbow tank will soon be torn down and the artwork transferred to the other tank.

Incongruously neighbored by huge cranes and warehouses, **Castle Island** is a windswept green park with a long promenade made for strolling. It's also the oldest continuously fortified site in North America. A fort, rebuilt several times, has stood here since 1634. The hilly lawns surrounding the high granite ramparts are a fine place to picnic. Edgar Allan Poe, who enlisted here, based his story "The Cask of Amontillado" on an incident that took place here, involving a young lieutenant, killed in a duel, whose friends sealed up the killer in one of the fort's lowest dungeons. Weekend tours of the fort are offered in the summer. The park is at the end of William J. Day Boulevard in South Boston; call (617) 727–5290.

One thing Boston is not noted for is beer. That situation is changing, however, with the 1985 introduction of Samuel Adams Boston Lager, the only American beer to pass Germany's strict, sixteenth-century beer purity law and the only American beer imported to and served in Germany. You can tour the Jamaica Plain brewery at 2:00 P.M. Thursday and Saturday, for a $1.00 donation, at 30 Germania Street, 1 block from the intersection of Washington and Boylston streets; call (617) 522–3400. After the tour, you'll see a short video and get to taste the line of beers and lagers, which include some seasonal varieties.

One of Boston's best-kept secrets is the **Boston Harbor Islands.** This group of some thirty islands scatters from Boston Harbor down the coast to Quincy and Hingham, accessible only by private boat or commercial ferry. Eight of them comprise a state park, with each island permeated by a unique flavor and character. The hub is Georges Island, where most ferries go first and where you can catch a free interisland summer water taxi. Exploring Civil War–era Fort Warren is the highlight of a trip to Georges Island, the most developed island. Peddocks Island, the largest, has a diverse terrain of woodlands, salt marsh, rocky beaches, and open fields. Tales of buried pirate treasure continue to surround Lovells Island, which also has a nice swimming beach. Berry-pickers love Grape Island, where they can gather raspberries, blackberries, and wild rose hips, meanwhile watching the wide variety of birds the berries attract. Bumpkin Island is known for its beautiful wildflowers; Great Brewster, for its profusion of wild roses. For information on Peddocks and Lovells islands, call the Boston Metropolitan District Commission's Harbor Region Office at (617) 727–5290. For Georges and the other islands, call the Boston Harbor Islands State Park in Hingham at (617) 740–1605.

To get to the islands, you can depart from Boston, Hingham, or Hull. Boston-based ferry services include Boston Harbor Cruises, at 1 Long Wharf (617–227–4321); Bay State Cruise Company, on Long Wharf (617–723–7800); and Massachusetts Bay Lines, at 60 Rowes Wharf (617–542–8000). The Friends of the Boston Harbor Islands sponsors special boat trips and tours, such as sunset cruises and trips to Boston Light, the nation's first lighthouse, on Little Brewster Island; call (617) 523–8386.

West of Boston

The famed architect of Boston's Emerald Necklace lived and worked on a quiet, tree-lined street in a Brookline neighborhood. His former home and office are now the **Frederick Law Olmsted National Historic Site,** holding photographs of his work and a vault full of thousands of his landscape plans. The rustically paneled second floor served as offices, but Olmsted, ever a lover of the outdoors, often took his desk out to a shady hollow in the yard to work. The house, located at 99 Warren Street, is open from 10:00 A.M. to 4:30 P.M. daily (last tour at 4:00). Call (617) 566–1689.

As you drive busy Route 16 in Waltham, you'd never know that just off it is a nineteenth-century country estate set in an oasis of green lawns, cornfields, and sheep pastures. One of the finest examples of Federal architecture in America, **Gore Place** was built in 1805 as the country seat for Christopher Gore, a wealthy lawyer who served as Massachusetts's first U.S. attorney in 1789, as well as state representative, U.S. senator, and governor. The symmetrical brick facade has a bowfront center flanked by two long wings, accented with lunette windows and black shutters. The Great Hall sets the tone, with its King of Prussia marble floor, 25-foot ceiling, and 3-story staircase that curves as gracefully as a swan's neck. Some of the furnishings are Gore family possessions, among them silver, crystal, and china, along with family portraits. One of the mansion's most unusual features is the Oval Drawing Room, an entirely oval room whose proportions echo those of the Roman Colosseum. Programs at Gore Place include summer concerts, a Christmas open house with period decorations, and an annual sheepshearing festival in April, complete with spinning and weaving demonstrations, crafts, folk music, and food. Two rotating exhibits a year relative to the Gore family and the period are displayed throughout the house. Gore Place is at 52 Gore Street; call (617) 894–2798. Hours are from 10:00 A.M. to 5:00 P.M. Tuesday through Saturday and from 2:00 to 5:00 P.M. (last tour at 4:00 P.M.) Sunday, from April 15 to November 15. Admission is $4.00 for adults and $2.00 for children.

The rural setting of the **DeCordova Museum** in Lincoln is a big attraction. Set in a wooded, green, thirty-acre park, it's a peaceful and uncrowded art museum to visit. Its holdings in twentieth-century American art include paintings, sculpture, graphics, and photography. The outdoor jazz concerts held in the summer are especially intimate gatherings. The museum also sponsors chamber music, ballet, modern dance, and rock music performances. The museum is on Sandy Pond Road; call (617) 259–8355. It's open from 10:00 A.M. to 5:00 P.M. Tuesday through Friday and from noon to 5:00 P.M. Sunday. Tickets to the museum cost $4.00.

Walter Gropius, founder of the Bauhaus school of art and architecture in Germany, designed and built his family home in the rolling green hills of Lincoln. **Gropius House** so perfectly embodied the Bauhaus principle of economy in design over ornamentation that it became much visited by architects. Industrial-style materials typical of Bauhaus style are seen in the glass block wall dividing the study and dining room and in the welded tubular steel staircase railing. Much of the furniture was designed by Gropius's friend Marcel Breuer. And Gropius's artist friends, among them Henry Moore, contributed works of art. The Gropius House, located at 68 Baker Bridge Road, is open from noon to 5:00 P.M. Friday through Sunday, June 1 to October 15; November 1 to May 30, it's open the first full weekend of the month. Call (617) 259–8843. Admission is $3.00.

If you'd like to explore the Lexington-Concord area, it would be hard to find a better base than the John David House, a bed-and-breakfast that opened in 1989 after a complete restoration. Built at the turn of the century, the house opens into a foyer of twin white-balustered staircases, accented by stunning red-patterned wallpaper. Four rooms all have private baths and are furnished with four-poster brass and mahogany beds, each graced with white eyelet spreads and pillow shams. Several rooms overlook the historic Lexington Battle Green. Afternoon tea is also included. Write the inn at 1963 Massachusetts Avenue, Lexington 02173, or call (617) 861–7376 (doubles, $85–$130).

Most likely, the Willow Pond Kitchen will stay the way it is until kingdom come—it's done so, at least, since about 1927. The ma-and-pa, down-home atmosphere walks on the wild side with its decor of moth-eaten stuffed bobcat, coyote, and even skunk. You sit at tacky Formica tables in ancient wooden booths where you are served great homemade food on paper plates. You can always count on lobster roll and lobster pie, steamed clams, and lots of fish dishes—also burgers, sandwiches, and homemade soups. The restaurant, at 745 Lexington Road in Concord, is open for lunch and dinner. Call (508) 369–6529.

Although Framingham is best known for its industry and mega-malls, it's also home to the **Garden in the Woods,** the largest landscaped collection of native plants and wildflowers in the Northeast. Woodland trails meander uphill and down, through such habitats as a lily pond, a rock garden, and a pine barren. The paths are well shaded by trees, which attract lots of songbirds to sweeten the walks. Rare and endangered plants are labeled. There's always something in bloom here, from yellow lady's slippers and trilliums in May to Turk's cap lilies and blazing stars in July and asters and gentians in the fall. The garden is on Hemenway Road; call (508) 877–6574 or (508) 877–7630. Admission is $5.00 for adults and $3.00 for children. The garden is open daily, except Mondays, from 9:00 A.M. to 4:00 P.M. mid-April through October.

North of Boston

More snowy owls congregate at Boston's Logan Airport than anywhere else in Massachusetts. From November to May, snowy owls migrate from their tundra habitats in Greenland, northern Canada, and Alaska to sit out the Arctic winter. To the owls, the vast landing fields of the airport look just like the tundra of home. As many as forty-three snowy owls have been banded here in one winter by the Massachusetts Audubon Society. Although you can't see the snowy owls at the airport, because no one is allowed out of doors, you can see them at Plum Island on the North Shore (see chapter 2).

Boston's Emerald Necklace is a postage-stamp park compared with the **Bay Circuit Trail.** First envisioned in 1929, the Bay Circuit is finally being implemented. It will run a ring of green 120 miles around Boston, linked by a scenic roadway and waterways. In its path will be some of New England's most traditional and scenic landscape: stone bridges, cart paths, small farms, fields lined with stone walls, brooks, salt marshes, and winding country lanes. Besides preserving the countryside, the Bay Circuit will include many cultural and historic attractions, such as the Castle Hill estate in Ipswich and Walden Pond in Concord. When it's done, sometime after the year 2000, it will be the state's most giant park and cultural attraction all in one—a museum of historic Massachusetts. The belt of green, which starts at Plum Island and swings west through Framingham and south to Kingston, includes fourteen state parks, as well as wetland and coastal areas that are home to hundreds of plant and animal species. In late 1990, the first section of the trail was dedicated in Boxford, a 12-mile stretch from a wildlife sanctuary to a state forest. Even though the Bay Circuit will be hemmed in between Route 128 and I–495, it will be a bastion against the explosive growth of metropolitan Boston. For more information, write the Bay Circuit Program, Department of Environmental Management, 100 Cambridge Street, Boston 02202, or call (617) 727–3160.

There are only three professional quilt museums in the United States, and one is in Lowell—the **New England Quilt Museum.** The seventy or so quilts in its permanent collection date back more than a hundred years. Rotating exhibits also showcase contemporary quilts, and the Christmas quilt show is especially colorful. The museum is in the Boott Mills Complex at the foot of John Street; call (508) 452–4207. Admission is $2.00. Hours are from 10:00 A.M. to 4:00 P.M. Tuesday through Saturday and from noon to 4:00 P.M. Sunday.

Off the Beaten Path on the North Shore

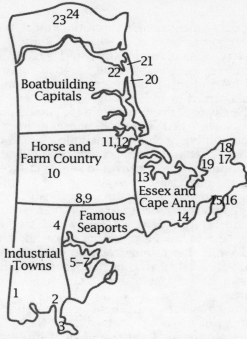

1. Saugus Iron Works National Historic Site
2. Lynn Historical Society
3. Nahant
4. Flash in the Pan Diner
5. Peabody Museum
6. Essex Institute
7. Chestnut Street
8. Wenham Tea House
9. Wenham Museum
10. Ipswich River Wildlife Sanctuary
11. Castle Hill
12. Goodale Orchards
13. Essex Shipbuilding Museum
14. Hammond Castle Museum
15. Cape Ann Historical Association
16. Beauport
17. Paper House
18. Halibut Point State Park
19. Annisquam
20. Parker River National Wildlife Refuge
21. Custom House Maritime Museum
22. Maudslay State Park
23. Lowell's Boat Shop
24. The Whittier Home

North Shore

It's ironic that most people's introduction to the North Shore of Boston comes by way of whizzing Route 1, arcadelike in its density of fast-food shops and gas stations and the famous fiberglass cows outside Saugus's Hilltop Steakhouse, for just beyond this urban surrealism lies some of the territory most prized by bluebloods, exclusive and expensive residential areas for Boston commuters. Three-hundred-year-old colonial towns with quaint seventeenth-century houses. Farmland and horse country, including a polo club in Hamilton where spectators throw champagne tailgate picnics and Princess Anne has been known to show her face.

Lining the coast all the way up to the Merrimac River and the New Hampshire border are seaports and fishing and boatbuilding capitals that became famous all over the world in the nineteenth century: Salem, Essex, Gloucester, and Newburyport. Serious yachters around the globe know of chichi Marblehead, which has a long tradition of maritime prowess—it was Marblehead men who ferried George Washington across the Delaware. And America's Cup contender Ted Hood makes sails here.

Magnificent white sand beaches stretch along miles of open ocean in Ipswich, Newbury, and Nahant. Cape Ann is known not only for fishing and boat building but for its artists' colonies, one of which is the oldest in the country.

But back to Route 1. Despite the fact that this is not the most attractive stretch you'll see in Massachusetts, it brings you to some interesting towns with industrial histories, among them Saugus, site of a Puritan ironworks, and Lynn, once known as "Shoe City." And you won't stand in line to see them.

For complete travel information, contact the North of Boston Convention and Visitors Council, P.O. Box 3031, Peabody 01960; (508) 745–2268.

Industrial Cities

Tucked away in Saugus is an unusual piece of history: the **Saugus Iron Works National Historic Site.** Here the Puritans built an ironworks in 1650 to supply the growing colony with nails and wrought iron previously shipped at great cost from England. The buildings have been faithfully recon- structed. Guided tours lead you from the two-story blast fur- nace, with its 18-foot bellows, to the forge, with its giant hammer and anvil, and to the rolling-and-slitting mill, where iron was flattened and cut for various products. The guide sets the waterwheel to turning, powering the blast furnace bellows. In the casting shed down below, it smells all dank and iron-y.

The site is so peaceful today that it's hard to imagine the hellish noise and heat the men worked in in those times. Now it looks like a green park. You might even see a snap- ping turtle laying its eggs on the slag heap, or a field of yel- low coreopsis in bloom. A nature trail winds along the Saugus River, once mighty enough to power seven water- wheels, now a tidal marsh. A museum holds artifacts found on the site and exhibits on the ironworks' history. There's also a tour of the seventeenth-century ironworks house. To get to the Central Street site, follow signs from either exit 43 off I–95 or the Main Street exit off Route 1. It's open from 9:00 A.M. to 5:00 P.M. daily; call (617) 233–0050.

The city of Lynn became a shoemaking center in the eigh- teenth century and was nationally known by the end of the 1800s. Shoemaking exhibits are displayed at the **Lynn His- torical Society** in a small yellow house on a quiet side street. Hanging on the wall is a large medallion under glass, almost 5 feet in diameter and made entirely of tiny shoe soles in concentric rings. The 234 soles, each unique to the maker, represented all the Lynn shoe manufacturers and dealers of the day at the 1893 Chicago Exposition. Ladies' turned shoes were Lynn's specialty; they were turned inside out to make the stitching fashionably invisible. Other exhibits are shoemakers' tools, antique clothes, postcards, and an 1896 switchboard. Lynn's 1860 shoemakers' strike made national news. A walking-tour brochure of some of the old shoe factories is available at the museum, at 125 Green Street. It's open from 1:00 to 4:00 P.M. Monday through Satur- day. Admission is $2.00 for adults and 50 cents for children. Call (617) 592–2465.

Poking southward from Lynn is a beach-flanked peninsula

called **Nahant** that in the nineteenth century was a classic seaside resort complete with grand hotels. A tour of Nahant makes a history-studded scenic drive. You can take either the Lynnway or Lynn Shore Drive to Nahant Road, which passes over a causeway to Nahant. On the left, you'll see Nahant Beach, a white crescent that attracted Boston Brahmins to build summer cottages. Among them were Cabots and Lodges, as well as Lowells and Lawrences, Harvard presidents, and judges and ambassadors. Another summer home belonged to "Ice King" Frederick Tudor, who cornered the ice market in Havana and Charleston by devising refrigerated boats. At 298 Nahant Road, Harriet Beecher Stowe summered. Henry Wadsworth Longfellow wrote part of *Hiawatha* in a boardinghouse at the corner of Willow and Wharf streets. Three presidents summered here too: Howard Taft and Teddy and Franklin D. Roosevelt. The first lawn tennis played in America was played here, at a Nahant country club in 1874. The 1823 Nahant Hotel was the first grand hotel of the country's first real summer colony.

Danvers is not a place you'd expect to find a gourmet restaurant. Nor would you expect to find gourmet food at a diner. But drive up shticky Route 1 north and you'll find them both at the **Flash in the Pan Diner,** a real diner complete with chrome walls and counter stools. And check out this menu: scampi pie and escargot pasta for appetizers; for dinner, marinated duckling, sea scallops and rock shrimp, and sirloin hearts with maple sugar and ginger. Desserts are special too: raspberry rhubarb bread pudding with whipped cream, Viennese lemon tart, and chocolate mousse cake. Call (508) 774–9367 for reservations (open for dinner only; closed Sunday and Monday).

Famous Seaports

Marblehead Harbor is one of the most beautiful harbors in New England. The fine shops and restaurants here, as well as three centuries of architecture that wind up and down the climbing narrow streets of its Old Town, draw big summer resort crowds. Still, there's no disputing the beauty of a drive out Marblehead Neck (take Pleasant Street to Ocean Avenue to reach the connecting causeway). The winding road passes a pretty beach and fantastic mansions, and then a stone castle. A sign on the right marks Castle Rock, where a short path leads to the rock, which you can climb for a gorgeous view of the coast. The road ends at Chandler Hovey Park, a pocket park high up that's a vantage point for stirring ocean views, and the Marblehead Light.

At a quiet remove from downtown is a splendid old English Tudor mansion cresting a seaside cliff, Spraycliff on the Ocean Bed and Breakfast. Guests can enjoy the ocean views from three terraces, one reached via a cliffside stairway, and from a private beach. The living room is light-filled, airy, and spacious. Seven guest rooms, each with private bath, are decorated in turn-of-the-century-seaside-resort style, with lots of wicker and chintz. Breakfast offers bounteous choices of breads and pastries, fresh fruit, and cereals. Spraycliff is located at 25 Spray Avenue, Marblehead (doubles, $95–$200). For reservations, write The Salem Inn, 7 Summer Street, Salem 01970, or call (508) 741–0680.

One of Marblehead's best-known restaurants is Rosalie's. In 1990 Rosalie's opened a sprightly basement cafe called Danielle's Cafe downstairs at Rosalie's. Young families, vacationers, and locals all break down the doors as soon as it opens at 5:00 P.M., lining up for great northern Italian fare at less than $10 an entree. Antipasti and *focaccia* complement the mouth-watering pizzas and pastas, such as *quattro formaggio* pizza and ziti Siciliano. The service is friendly and the ambience chic: painted bowls of crayon-colored fruits and a splash of neon dance up the wall and tablecloth designs. The young wait staff dress like New Kids on the Block. The restaurant, at 20 Sewall Street, serves dinner only. Call (617) 631–5353.

Salem is so filled with maritime history that you could easily spend a week here. Boosted by its maritime trade, Salem was once the nation's sixth-largest city. By 1800, so many Salem ships filled Asian ports that some traders thought Salem was a country. Early on, sea captains knew they were bringing home rare oddities, and in 1799 they founded the East India Marine Society, a "museum of natural and artificial curiosities." The original 1824 granite building with a black anchor in front has grown into the **Peabody Museum,** the oldest continuously operating museum in America. It also must be the most treasure-filled maritime museum in all of New England. Thirty brightly designed galleries hold maritime artifacts, Asian export art, and exhibits in ethnology, natural history, and archaeology. Among the "curiosities" you'll encounter are a ship's model made entirely of cloves, a 6-inch-tall hair comb elaborately carved from a single scale of a Pacific tortoise, and a stuffed scarlet ibis from Brazil. Ships' figureheads and paintings of Salem ships and Chinese ports feature prominently, as do exotic treasures from Bombay to Zanzibar. Asian export art made just for trade with the West includes engraved silver teapots, a secretary made entirely of carved ivory, and a Chinese "moon bed" whose oval-shaped, dark wood canopy is inlaid with ivory and cut out with hundreds of infinitesimally small designs of people, pagodas, and boats. The museum is in East India Square, downtown in the Essex Street Mall; call (508) 745–1876. Hours are 10:00 A.M. to 5:00 P.M. Monday through Saturday and from noon on Sunday. Admission is $4.00 for adults and $1.50 for children.

Across the mall at the **Essex Institute** (508–744–3390), period houses on landscaped grounds span three centuries of architecture. The 1804 Gardner-Pingree House, considered the masterpiece of famed Salem architect Samuel McIntire, has elaborate details. Door and window corners are carved with sheaves of wheat—symbols of prosperity—and there are painted floor cloths and Adams-style marble mantelpieces. Museum holdings, in a beautiful gallery with white Corinthian columns and a vaulted ceiling, feature oil portraits of such leading figures as Nathaniel Hawthorne and Daniel Webster, as well as period silver pieces. Also among the collections are hundreds of pieces of eighteenth- and nineteenth-century European porcelain and glassware. Hours are 10:00 A.M. to 5:00 P.M. Tuesday through Sunday (museum only) and noon to 5:00 P.M. weekends (houses and museum). The museum is also open Mondays in summer; hours are reduced in winter. Admission to the museum is $4.00 for adults and $2.50 for children. On weekends, admission to the museum and period houses is $6.00 for adults and $3.50 for children.

Magnificent and stately sea captains' houses line the entire length of quiet, tree-shaded **Chestnut Street,** just west of the Essex Street Mall. Federal-style temples to wealth stand in neat rows, painted in pastels of creamy yellow, white, or taupe. Wonderful period details stand out: a gold eagle medallion over a door, urn-topped fence posts, fanlight windows, white pillared porticoes, and tidy black shutters.

Diners find live piano music and excellent grilled fresh fish at The Lyceum, located at 43 Church Street (508–745–7665), in the heart of the Essex Street Mall. In the 1840s the brick, Federal building with fanlight windows was a lecture hall, where Hawthorne, Emerson, and Thoreau consorted. And Alexander Graham Bell made his first public demonstration of the telephone here in 1877.

Down near the waterfront, The Grapevine, at 26 Congress Street (508–745–9335), offers an Italian-inspired seafood and pasta menu, rounded out with *pizzettas* and meats. An enchanting alfresco patio reminds one of Florence. (The restaurant is open for lunch and dinner.)

Horse and Farm Country

A genteel atmosphere of yesteryear still lingers at the **Wenham Tea House,** which opened in 1910 as a fund-raising arm of the Wenham Village Improvement Society. Ladies brought their daughters for birthdays and bridal showers to the tearoom with its painted yellow chairs and flowered curtains. Tea, served from 3:15 to 4:30 P.M., is a delicious affair of scones with whipped cream and raspberry jam, cinnamon sticks, and afternoon tea bread. Dainty and traditional lunches include creamed chicken on toast, lobster roll, and cottage cheese with fruit. A really nice gift shop sells jams, teas, cookies, and candies; a profusion of books on gardening, cooking, birds, and travel; and such handcrafts and housewares as Waterford crystal, silver, handbags, and painted ceramics. The teahouse, on Route 1A in the center of Wenham, is closed on Sundays. Reservations are recommended; call (508) 468–1398.

Right across the street is the **Wenham Museum,** at 132 Main Street (508–468–2377), offering a fantastic collection of dolls—unique, unusual, and antique ones. Besides nineteenth-century German bisque-head dolls and Kewpie dolls, you'll find an Eskimo doll carved of walrus tusk and only 1.75 inches tall, a 1797 "penny" wooden doll, and an Egyptian doll that dates to 1200 B.C. There are dolls from around the world—Sweden, Russia, and Portugal, and Hopi *kachina* dolls. Some quirky ones are dolls of the Dionne quintuplets and dolls representing the television Addams Family. Also part of the museum is the historic Claflin-Richards House, dating to 1660 and characteristic of an English house of that period. Last but not least, Wenham's nineteenth-century ice industry is chronicled. So famed for purity and long lastingness was Wenham ice that it was shipped to India, the West Indies, and England; Queen Victoria served it at Buckingham Palace. The Wenham Museum is open from 11:00 A.M. to 4:00 P.M. weekdays, from 1:00 P.M. Saturday, and from 2:00 to 5:00 P.M. Sunday. Admission is $2.00 for adults and 75 cents for children.

The **Ipswich River Wildlife Sanctuary** is Massachusetts Audubon's largest. The property is remote and wild: 2,000 acres of meadow, swamp, ponds, drumlins, kettle holes, and eskers surrounding the Ipswich River. Highlights are an unusual rockery, waterfowl ponds, and an observation tower overlooking swamp and meadowland. One of the buildings has a long and narrow bird-viewing window high up, from which you can see many birds at a profusion of feeders in the backyard. Programs include guided river float trips, maple sugaring, canoe rentals, cabin rental and camping on Perkins Island, and many nature programs for children. The sanctuary is located on Perkins Row in Topsfield, just off Route 97 east from Route 1. It's closed Mondays. There's a $3.00 trail fee for adults. Call (508) 887–9264.

One of the most splendid estates in all of Massachusetts is on Argilla Road in Ipswich. This fifty-nine-room seaside mansion was built by Chicago industrialist Richard T. Crane, Jr., whose father made a fortune in plumbing valves and fittings. Crane succeeded his father as president in 1914 and also made the company famous for elegant bathroom fixtures in the 1920s, partly by advertising them in *National Geographic.* Built in 1927, **Castle Hill** was a summer home for Crane and his wife. Touring the mansion is like touring one of the great castles of Europe. A long drive winds up and up through the landscaped grounds, past the stone walls and balusters of a sunken Italian garden and a rose garden. The mansion's long symmetrical lines reflect great seventeenth-century English houses of the Stuart style. Inside you find yourself staring up at 16-foot ceilings and elaborately carved ceiling moldings, marveling at serpentine marble fireplaces and crystal and brass chandeliers, and noticing such exquisite details as delft tiling, parquet floors, and sterling-silver bathroom fixtures. Bay windows in many rooms offer sweeping views of the barrier beach and the ocean down below and of the green lawns of the grounds. A particularly striking view is of the Grand Allée, which slopes down a wide path straight to the sea. Lined with spruce trees and stone garden statuary, the *allée* was the site of a casino used for summer parties and of a saltwater swimming pool, now filled in. One terraced lawn was formerly a bowling lawn; another held a classically designed boxwood maze.

Inside, the entrance rotunda offers an unusual example of circular architecture. Its round surfaces are covered with canvas painted with murals of Roman emperors, Corinthian columns, and the Crane children, Florence and Cornelius. You can see most of the house on the tour, from the 63-foot gallery to the dining room, kitchens, and guest and family bedrooms and bathrooms. The library was taken entirely from an English estate in Hertfordshire. Warm and rich wood paneling culminates in ornately carved fruits and flowers framing a doorway and several paintings, the work of famed seventeenth-century English craftsman Grinling Gibbons. Surrounding the bathtub in daughter Florence's bathroom is a striking mosaic of reverse-painted glass tiles in a black clipper-ship motif framed in silver. Mrs. Crane's bathroom was done entirely in green-and-white serpentine marble and *faux marbre*. The green marble was designed to make the bathwater look like seawater.

The house is opened four times a year for public tours, once each season. Tickets cost $5.00 for adults and $3.00 for children. Appointments can also be made for groups. Call (508) 356–4351 for tour dates and information. Castle Hill also hosts summer concerts and other special programs on its beautiful grounds, events that sometimes include preliminary house tours. Picnicking on the Grand Allée before a summer concert is a popular activity. Visitors are welcome to stroll the lovely grounds anytime there is not a private function.

Just below Castle Hill, at the foot of Argilla Road, is one of the North Shore's most magnificent beaches: Crane Beach, once part of the Crane estate. A white sandy beach stretches more than 4 miles long, reaching down from a scenic sweep of dunes and marsh grasses and a view of the Ipswich River. There are bathhouses and a snack bar. Parking fees are stiff: $10.00 on weekends and $6.00 during the week, except Monday and Tuesday, when the price dips to $3.00. (The stiffer fees are half-price after 3 P.M.) For information, call (508) 356–4354.

On your way back from the beach, be sure to stop at **Goodale Orchards** on the left, at 123 Argilla Road (508–356–5366). This is a great old-fashioned barn of a place, famous for its homemade cider doughnuts. Come fall, the doughnuts can be washed down with cider, stocked in three antique white refrigerators. The barn rambles back forever, and its rafters are piled high with old wooden bushel baskets. It smells perennially of good things: homemade fruit pies, newly harvested berries, jams and jellies, stick candy, vegetables, and cut flowers. Children love the place for the hayrides and farm animals—the pig, goats, geese, ducks, chickens, and horses.

Essex and Cape Ann

At the entrance to Cape Ann, the town of Essex is well known as an antiques capital. What is typically overlooked here is the **Essex Shipbuilding Museum,** though it is in the thick of the antiques shops, right on Main Street (Route 133). Into this small but fascinating museum is crammed a great amount of artifacts and photos illustrating Essex's 300-year shipbuilding history, during which more than 4,000 ships were built. Essex became famous for its Chebacco Dogbody boat, a two-masted fishing boat designed to be built quickly to help replace New England's fishing fleet after it was destroyed by the British. There are models of schooners with beautiful linen sails, as well as many half-models, used in boat design, their lines judged for speed and seaworthiness.

Near a workbench with antique tools is an 1890s trunnel lathe, used to make trunnels (tree nails, or wooden nails). The appealing smells of oakum (tarred hemp) and pine pitch permeate the caulking exhibit. Everything for Essex ships was made in town: windlasses, blocks, pumps, sparks, cordage, anchors, sails, and riggings. Museum hours are 11:00 A.M. to 4:00 P.M. Thursday through Sunday from Memorial Day to Columbus Day. Tickets cost $2.00. Call (508) 768–7541.

Hammond Castle Museum looks just like a real castle. Its stone battlements and towers, built right on the rocky shores of the Atlantic Ocean, house one of the most unusual private homes in America. The castle is a fitting monument to the man who built it, Dr. John Hays Hammond, Jr., America's second-greatest inventor, next to Thomas Edison. When he died in 1965, Hammond held 465 patents resulting from more than 800 inventions. He collected monuments all through Europe, such items as Roman tombstones, Renaissance furniture, and a medieval fireplace. To house it all, he built his castle in the 1920s.

Tours begin in the thirteenth-century-style Great Hall, whose 60-foot ceiling complements an 8,200-pipe organ, the largest organ in the world installed in a private home. You walk in accompanied by the imposing strains of this organ—quite an effect. The walls surrounding the courtyard and pool are made of half-timbered shop facades from a fourteenth-century French village: a bakeshop, wine merchant, and butcher, complete with symbols for the illiterate. A church front holds Hammond's collection of Roman tombstones set into the wall. There's also a Renaissance dining room, along with Gothic and early American bedrooms. The lobby contains a list of Hammond's patents and exhibits some of his patent models. An "inventor's inventor," Hammond pioneered in radio, television, radar, and remote-control radio. Hammond and his wife entertained Serge Koussevitzky, Helen Hayes, George Gershwin, Cole Porter, John D. Rockefeller, and Noel Coward, as well as Ethel and Lionel Barrymore, who staged readings of Shakespeare in the Great Hall. The museum is open from 9:00 A.M. to 5:00 P.M. Tuesday through Sunday. It's located at 80 Hesperus Avenue, Gloucester; call (508) 283–7673 or (800) 649–1930 (in Massachusetts). Tickets cost $5.00 for adults and $3.00 for children. A wide array of organ concerts and programs is held year-round.

The marine heart and soul of Gloucester shows at the **Cape Ann Historical Association,** starting with the nation's largest collection of paintings and drawings by Fitz Hugh Lane. A Gloucester native, Lane was the first American marine painter to win stature. His scenes of Gloucester Harbor and other shores in New England are full of light and sky. Decorative arts exhibits include Queen Anne and Hepplewhite furniture. Upstairs are fisheries exhibits. Long oars, painted in bright colors and carried in the annual Saint Peter's Fiesta, hang on the wall. A flake yard shows how fish was salted and dried years ago. Connected to the museum and part of the tour is an 1804 Federal-style sea captain's house, the Captain Elias Davis House. The museum is located at 27 Pleasant Street; call (508) 283-0455. Hours are 10:00 A.M. to 5:00 P.M. Tuesday through Saturday. Admission is $3.00 for adults.

In Gloucester quite a lot of mediocre seafood is dished up to tourists in the name of the real thing. For better choices, try these: (1). Barish's Restaurant, at 110 Main Street (508–281–1911), is a homey-feeling lace-curtained bistro that serves rustic and spicy Italian and French country food with real imagination and special touches. The garlic bread is made with sun-dried tomatoes; the house salad, of radicchio with goat cheese and walnuts. Dishes might include tenderloin, served with a pureed roast pepper sauce, Roquefort cheese, and grilled leeks, and beggar's pockets—Italian dumplings stuffed with meat and grilled with a marinara sauce and cheese. The restaurant is open for lunch and dinner and is somewhat expensive but worth it.

(2). At Boulevard Ocean View Restaurant, at 25 Western Avenue (508–281–2949), Portuguese food is the specialty. Though the dining room is small and noisy, it's a friendly place for enjoying excellent kale soup, paella, and *mascareda,* a Portuguese version of bouillabaisse. It's open for lunch and dinner and also for breakfast on weekends.

(3). The Rudder, at 73 Rocky Neck Avenue (508–283–7967), is a real institution, Gloucester's oldest restaurant. It's situated out on Rocky Neck, America's oldest art colony, and dinner or drinks here is a nice way to cap a day spent gallery hopping. Housed in a 175-year-old former fish-packing shed right on the water, the dining room is all dark wood and brass lanterns. An oceanfront porch opens up for summertime dining. The chief attraction is not so much the food, although the variety of seafood is well prepared, as the "spontaneous entertainment" provided by its theatrically minded family owners. They are likely to flit about the dining room or accompany themselves in an impromptu number on the piano every night. A "celebrity wall" holds photos of famous guests: Liv Ullmann, Anthony Newley, Judy Garland. The ceiling is plastered with menus from restaurants around the world, collected by the owners' many globetrotting friends.

Out on Gloucester's exclusive Eastern Point is one of the most intriguing houses you'll ever see: **Beauport.** This rambling shingled-and-turreted house was built in 1907 by the daring interior designer Henry Davis Sleeper, who numbered among his clients Henry Francis du Pont, Joan Crawford, and Fredric March. Sleeper collected pieces of decorative arts and then ran out of room to display them in his three-room house. He began adding on, and kept adding on, for more than twenty-six years, until his death in 1934. The final fantastic product has twenty-two different roof levels and more than forty rooms. Without a guide, you could get lost wandering these cramped and dark little rooms that honeycomb throughout the house, occasionally opening on only a peek of a view of Gloucester Harbor. Sleeper built secret staircases, fake windows, and doors to nowhere. He indulged his every fancy. He built shrines to the American colonial past, honoring George Washington and Benjamin Franklin. The China Trade Room started as a medieval hall until Sleeper acquired some hand-painted eighteenth-century Chinese wallpaper. The wallpaper's large murals show village scenes in China. The Chinese theme is completed with a Chinese pagoda–shaped ceiling and a Buddha in the fireplace. The Octagon Room has octagonal sides and contains a collection of eight-sided antiques. A guest room called the Strawberry Hill Room is done with a strawberry theme, vaulted ceiling, and red-and-black lacquered wallpaper of elephants and camels. Beauport is at 75 Eastern Point Boulevard (this is a private road but open to visitors to Beauport). Admission for

adults is $5.00; for children, $2.50. The house is open from
10:00 A.M. to 4:00 P.M. weekdays from May 15 through mid-
September and also from 1:00 to 4:00 P.M. weekends thereafter until October 15. Call (508) 283–0800 for information.

We all have our curiosities. Elis Stenman of Rockport wanted
to see how far you could push newspapers without destroying
the print. Accordingly, he built a house out of them, starting
in 1922, and the structure is still standing today—the **Paper
House.** The two-room house has walls made of 215 thick-
nesses of newsprint and contains furniture made of rolled-up
newspapers. You can still read the print under the shellac. A
desk gives an account of Charles Lindbergh's historic flight. A
grandfather clock made in 1932 contains papers from the
capital cities of forty-eight states. The mantel is made of Sunday rotogravure sections. Stenman and his wife used the
house and its furniture for four summers. The house is
located at 52 Pigeon Hill Street. Take Route 127 north to Curtis Street; then follow signs to the Paper House. It's open daily
from 10:00 A.M. to 5:00 P.M. in July and August and can be
seen by appointment in spring and fall; call (508) 546–2629.
Admission is $1.00 for adults and 50 cents for children.

At the northernmost tip of Cape Ann is an old quarry site
that is now **Halibut Point State Park,** a small but special
park. A film at the visitor center tells the story of how granite
was king here for almost a hundred years. Paving blocks
went to Boston, Philadelphia, New York, and Havana. Halibut
Point granite blocks were used in Boston's Custom House
tower, the Brooklyn Bridge, and the Holland Tunnel. A self-
guided trail passes by the vestiges of quarrying, coming out
on a stunning vantage point overlooking a quarry pool high
up over the Atlantic Ocean. This is also a great place for bird-
watching; hundreds of species have been sighted. Saturday
morning guided tours are offered from 9:30 to 11:30 A.M.
from late May to Columbus Day (a $5.00 parking fee is
charged during these months). The visitor center is open
from 8:00 A.M. to 6:00 P.M. in summer and closes at 4:00 P.M.
in winter. Call (508) 546–2997.

If you'd like to stay at a place that's handy to Halibut Point,
try the Old Farm Inn, right next door. A rambling old red
farmhouse set way back behind a stone wall, the Old Farm
Inn is a real farmhouse that dates to about 1799 and once

Annisquam Footbridge

housed granite workers from the Halibut Point Quarry. At a distance from Rockport Center, it's a restful alternative to the crowds and noise of downtown Rockport. The country decor includes original gunstock beams, handmade quilts, and braided rugs. Breakfast is served in a glassed-in sun room overlooking the landscaped grounds. For reservations, write the inn at 291 Granite Street, Rockport 01966, or call (508) 546–3237 (doubles, $65–$98).

If you keep following Route 127 around the back side of Cape Ann, it goes to **Annisquam,** a remote village that was a fishing and boatbuilding center for more than two and a half centuries. Annisquam is tiny, with just a few narrow streets hemming the ocean, winding uphill and down. The people who live here have stately ocean views from their attractive Victorian shingled and wooden saltbox houses. The Annisquam Yacht Club is unusual, built out on the water on stilts. The old wooden footbridge crossing Lobster Cove is a nice place to stroll and admire the cove.

Historic Boat-building Towns

Plum Island, which juts south more than 6 miles into the Atlantic, is the site of one of the best birding spots on the East Coast, the **Parker River National Wildlife Refuge,** one of the last undeveloped barrier beaches. More than 300 species have been sighted here. The spectacular scenery encompasses 5,000 acres of wide sandy beach, dunes, bogs, freshwater pools, and tidal marshes reaching into river and ocean. Boardwalks lead to the beach, and there are several nature trails, observation towers, and camera blinds. Because this is a very popular place, the best time to come is off-season. Another good reason to come off-season is that the beach is closed to people from April until July or August, to allow the endangered piping plover to nest and fledge its young undisturbed. The rest of the refuge is open for birding, biking, hiking, and nonbeach recreation. You'll find something happening and something to see every month. In November and December, you can see migrating Canada and snow geese; January brings snowy owls; and you can pick wild beach plums and cranberries in September and October (within limits). Call (508) 465–5753 for information. Admission is $5.00 per car and $1.00 per pedestrian or bicyclist. Park headquarters is at the northern end of the island and is open from 8:00 A.M. to 4:30 P.M. weekdays. To get there, follow signs from Route 1A, approaching Newburyport.

The city of Newburyport is one of the most attractive along the coast. Along High Street (Route 1A) stand dozens of sea captains' houses, ranging from Greek Revival and Federal to Georgian and Victorian, some with cupolas and widow's walks. Downtown, nineteenth-century brick commercial buildings in Market Square have been made into a handsome shopping and dining complex, gracefully accented with cobblestone sidewalks; black iron, gas-style street lamps; and lots of trees and potted geraniums.

A hop, skip, and a jump away, at 25 Water Street, is the **Custom House Maritime Museum,** whose collections are beautifully set off in the classic 1835 Greek Revival granite structure. Its small rooms still have their original vaulted ceilings, brick floors, marble windowsills, and wide, tall windows. A cantilevered granite stairway leads to the second

38

floor. Newburyport is the birthplace of the U.S. Coast Guard, and the first revenue cutters were built here by Newburyport shipwrights. The office of the collector of customs holds chests of Ceylon tea, barrels of rum, and lacquered boxes. There are antiques and oil portraits memorializing shipping families, as well as many other maritime memorabilia. The museum is open from 10:00 A.M. to 4:00 P.M. Monday through Saturday and from 1:00 P.M. to 4:00 P.M. Sunday. Tickets cost $3.00 for adults and $1.50 for children. Call (508) 462–8681.

Although Market Square is full of restaurants, one that locals prefer is Middle Street Foods (508–465–8333), 2 blocks up at 25 Middle Street, off State Street. This is such a tiny place that it's geared more to takeout, but the food is delicious and all homemade from scratch. The outstanding pastries and desserts include scones, coffee cakes, banana caramel tart, and a six-layer chocolate cake. Overstuffed deli sandwiches and such homemade soups as carrot-orange-ginger are popular, as are the daily changing entrees, such as spinach and bacon tart and turkey potpie. An outdoor brick patio opens in warm weather.

Hidden away from downtown Newburyport is **Maudslay State Park,** acquired in 1985. Once the private estate of a wealthy family, the property retains its beautifully landscaped grounds, carriage roads, and trails. Enormous rhodedenrons rise over your head along the paths, as do centuries-old stands of laurel, one of New England's largest natural stands. Although the mansions are gone, there are still an *allée* of red oak, the stone foundations of greenhouses, and the foundations of a formal Italian garden and a rose garden. A walk through the woods brings you to a large clearing on a rise, offering a stunning view of the Merrimac River. Lots of special programs and arts performances take place in the park, including autumn hayrides and children's outdoor theater. In winter, cross-country skiing here is pleasant. The park is on Curzon's Mill Road. From Route 113 east, take a left onto Noble Street and follow signs. Call (508) 465–7223.

Sleepy little Amesbury is so far off the beaten path that few people come here. But they're missing **Lowell's Boat Shop,** which dates to 1793 and is still making handmade wooden boats on the original site. Now a National Historic Landmark, the shop was founded by the Lowell family, who owned and ran it for seven generations, until 1976. In 1793, Simeon Lowell found boats unseaworthy for the three-knot current at the mouth of the Merrimac River. He designed himself a boat that would not capsize and that would be rowable in this heavy surf: a double-ended lapstrake skiff with a raked transom. The world-famous design was called the Amesbury skiff, or dory. Thousands were made for Grand Banks schooners, the U.S. Life Saving Service (forerunner of the Coast Guard), the army and Navy in World War II, and early nineteenth-century pleasure boaters.

The shop still looks as it did 200 years ago, sitting right on the banks of the Merrimac River. Only a wood stove heats the wooden building, which smells of sawdust and spar varnish. Downstairs in the paint shop, paint drippings of centuries are so thick—some 7 inches deep—that the floor looks paved. Amesbury skiffs are still handmade exactly the way they were in 1793, of hand-cut white oak, mahogany, and pine. It takes almost two months to build a boat, and orders come from as far as California, Florida, and Africa. You can visit the shop during business hours—from 7:30 A.M. to 5:00 P.M. weekdays—if you call ahead. The shop is at 459 Main Street; call (508) 388–0162.

John Greenleaf Whittier lived in Amesbury for fifty-six years, until his death in 1892. **The Whittier Home** is entirely furnished with this Quaker poet and abolitionist's belongings and books. A white frame house with a picket fence, it has small, cozy rooms done in simple country style. Whittier, who never married, lived here with the female triumvirate of his mother, sister, and aunt. Memorabilia include the desk where he wrote his famous poem *Snow-Bound* and his newspaper-lined traveling case. The Garden Room, where he did most of his writing, has his wood stove and divan in place, and the room's walls are full of pictures of his favorite writers. His boots stand on the floor, and his shawl and hat are draped on the rocker. The home, at 86 Friend Street, is open from 10:00 A.M. to 4:00 P.M. Tuesday through Saturday, May 1 to October 31. Fees are $2.00 for adults and 50 cents for children. Call (508) 388–1337.

Off the Beaten Path on the South Shore

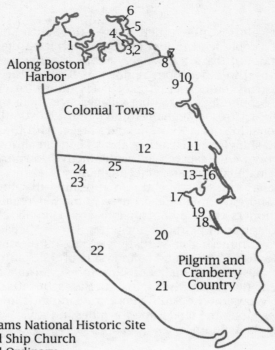

1. Adams National Historic Site
2. Old Ship Church
3. Old Ordinary
4. World's End
5. Carousel under the Clock
6. Hull Lifesaving Museum
7. Jerusalem Road
8. Carillon concert series
9. Lawson Tower
10. Scituate Lighthouse
11. Winslow House
12. Herring Run Park
13. John Alden House
14. Art Complex Museum
15. French Memories Bakery
16. King Caesar House
17. Persy's Place
18. Whale Discovery Center
19. Capt. John Boats
20. Cranberry harvest
21. Edaville Railroad
22. Middleborough
    Historical Museum
23. Elmwood Post Office
24. Joppa Grill
25. Phil's Family Restaurant

South Shore

You might call Boston's "other" shore—the South Shore—a black hole. People tend to just drive through it on their way to Cape Cod. But that's a mistake. Snubbed as the least preferred of the three bedroom regions of Boston, the South Shore is a truly hidden area, except Plymouth, of course. Colonial shipbuilding and fishing villages stretch all the way along the coast from Hingham to Plymouth. Most still have the traditional look of a New England village, with the pretty saltbox and shingled houses they always had. Small-town life is remarkably well preserved in the distinctive downtowns of Cohasset, Duxbury, Scituate, and Hingham.

The beaches and coastline are so appealing that much of the South Shore became a resort area in the nineteenth century. Vacationers came by steamer to grand hotels in Hull. Wealthy Boston Irish politicos, including James Michael Curley, took to summering in Scituate, yielding its nickname of "the Irish Riviera." The inland countryside of the South Shore offers countless scenic vistas of pine forest, farmland, and the banks of the North River. Most of Massachusetts's cranberry crop grows on the South Shore, spreading its low-lying russet vines along the landscape for miles in Carver, Middleborough, and Plymouth.

Along Boston Harbor

Though tourists usually bypass Quincy, it's the only American city that was home to two U.S. presidents, John Adams and John Quincy Adams. You can see the family home to four generations of Adamses at the **Adams National Historic Site.** It's hard to picture this stately gray house surrounded by farmland, gardens, and orchards as it was when John and his wife, Abigail, moved in, in 1788. While John pursued his duties in Washington, Abigail busied herself tending the farm and adding a new wing to the house. Family possessions give a deep sense of how loved and used the house was as a family seat. A good-luck horseshoe hangs over the door where

Abigail placed it. The wing chair that John Adams died in is still there. Waterford crystal bowls in a china closet are cracked because John Adams sprouted seeds in them. The lovely landscaped grounds hold formal gardens, lilacs with waist-thick trunks, and climbing wisteria. The site, at 135 Adams Street, is open daily from 9:00 A.M. to 5:00 P.M. April 19 to November 10. Call (617) 773–1177. Your $2.00 ticket also admits you to the nearby Adams Birthplaces on Franklin Street, where John Adams and John Quincy Adams were born.

If you head south on Route 3A, it will take you the whole length of the coastal South Shore. First stop is Hingham, a colonial town whose Main Street (Route 228) Eleanor Roosevelt called "the most beautiful Main Street in America." This wide, tree-lined boulevard is an oasis of restored homes spanning three centuries. Downtown Hingham has a wealth of historic sights, unique among them the **Old Ship Church** (617– 749–1679), America's oldest continuously operating church, since 1681. It's one of the few Elizabethan structures left in New England. Ship's carpenters made its lofty ceiling like an upside-down ship's keel. The church is at 90 Main Street.

Just beyond Hingham Square, at 21 Lincoln Street, you'll find the **Old Ordinary,** once a seventeenth-century hostelry and now a museum of Hingham history. As a tavern, the Ordinary served an "ordinary meal of the day" to travelers. The taproom looks just as it did, with bar and wooden grille, wooden kegs, and copper tankards. An eighteenth-century parlor, kitchen, dining room, tool room, and small library are furnished with period antiques. Upstairs, bedrooms display memorabilia of local families and some rare silk mourning samplers. The museum is open from 1:30 to 4:30 P.M. mid-June to Labor Day. Admission is $2.00 for adults and 50 cents for children. For information, call the Hingham Historical Society at (617) 749–7721.

Across the street from the Old Ordinary is a small green park with a statue of Abraham Lincoln. Abraham Lincoln's ancestor Samuel Lincoln hailed from Hingham.

At lunchtime, make tracks for The British Relief, at 152 North Street in Hingham Square (617–749–7713). This is one of those homey eateries where everyone feels welcome. Housed in a red brick storefront, the restaurant has comfortable wooden booths and tables and a massive carved oak table that seats ten. Cafeteria-style service dishes up outstanding breakfasts and lunches, including homemade muffins and coffee cakes, hearty homemade soups, salads, sandwiches, and desserts.

Also in Hingham is one of the South Shore's nicest parks, **World's End.** Planned as a housing subdivision in the nineteenth century, World's End has wide *allées* designed by Frederick Law Olmsted. The paths sweep uphill to stunning views of the Boston skyline, especially at sunset. To get there, go straight through the rotary on Route 3A south onto Summer Street, and turn left onto Martin's Lane. Call (508) 921–1944 or (617) 749–8956. Admission is $2.00.

There's only one bed-and-breakfast in historic-district-minded Hingham. It's the Ripley House, one of the lovely old houses along Main Street. The 1691 home still has its original wide-planked, honey-pine floors, now polished to a fine sheen. A former keeping room has one corner made of brick to house an iron kettle. A large living room meanders through the period-furnished breakfast room to an upstairs library nook. Guest rooms have fireplaces and are done up with antiques, handmade quilts, feather beds, and floral wallpapers. For reservations, write the establishment at 347 Main Street, Hingham 02043, or call (617) 749–7011 (doubles, $55–$65; baths are shared).

At the turn of the century, Hull was a stylish resort, complete with grand hotels and an amusement park with a roller coaster. Bathing-costumed vacationers sought summer relief on the miles of white sand and surf at Nantasket Beach, one of the largest beaches on the South Shore. In later decades, Hull deteriorated into a more honky-tonk atmosphere. But the town is once again metamorphosing into a sparkling place, spurred by an arts community.

One vestige of the amusement park that still charms is the vintage 1928 **Carousel under the Clock,** across the street from the beach in a wooden pavilion under an antique clock tower. A ride on the carousel is magic in summer. Infectious antique pipe organ music pumps away, the lights shine, and a breeze from the beach sweeps in through the open doors. Brightly painted horses and mermaid-bedecked chariots ferry you around in season. Call (617) 925–0472 for information.

Nantasket Avenue, Hull's main street, takes you out to the

Hull Lifesaving Museum

Hull Lifesaving Museum, an engaging place that recreates the days of valiant surfmen and tragic shipwrecks. The bare wood walls of the station show the spartan surroundings the surfmen lived in a hundred years ago. They drilled every day, practicing with the breeches buoy, boat launchings, capsizing, and resuscitation. You can tour the galley, an equipment room, and the bedroom of Captain Joshua James, the station's first captain. Dedicating his life to rescues at sea after his mother and baby sister drowned at sea, James became the nation's most decorated lifesaver, rescuing more than 540 people from eighty-six wrecks. When this station opened, in 1889, it was the first official lifesaving service in America. There are lots of memorabilia and photos to look at, as well as a breeches buoy and faking box. In the boat house you can admire a hundred-year-old surfboat with 16-foot pulling oars. A ladder climbs up to the lookout tower. The museum, at 1117 Nantasket Avenue, is open Wednesday through Sunday from noon to 5:00 P.M. in July and August and only on weekends and Monday holidays in the off-season. Admission is $2.00 for adults and $1.00 for children over five. Call (617) 925–5433.

Up behind the Hull Lifesaving Museum, you can climb Telegraph Hill, the highest point on the South Shore, for a splendid view of Hull Harbor and the Atlantic Ocean. Though now it's covered with graffiti, the stone, revolutionary war–era Fort Revere has the distinction of having been fired on by the British.

An unusual restaurant find in this beach town is Saporito's Florence Club Cafe (617–925–3023), a gourmet Italian restaurant where the food is so good that it lets the South Shore thumb its nose at Boston's North End. Well disguised inside a beat-up, 1940 Italian club is a gardeny Florentine retreat done up in turquoise and peach, plus white latticework. The mouth-watering food includes such intriguing appetizers as grilled *pizzettas*—perhaps topped with lamb, veal, sausage, red and yellow peppers, and feta—and seafood, meats, and pastas in original sauces, such as *pappardelle* with grilled shrimp, grilled leeks, lobster sauce, and basil. Saporito's is at 11 Rockland Circle; call (617) 925–3023. It's open for dinner only and is closed Mondays.

Colonial Towns

Newport has Ocean Drive. Cohasset has **Jerusalem Road.** This scenic drive winds between Route 228 and North Main Street along rocky coast and secluded beaches, past million-dollar houses perched perilously close to the sea. Offshore, the tall granite spire is Minot's Light, whose famous signal flashes I-LOVE-YOU.

Downtown Cohasset has a classic town green with a duck pond and white-steepled church. At the other end stands a tall granite church, Saint Stephen's. This church is home to the oldest running **carillon concert series** in North America, begun in 1924. Its fifty-seven-bell carillon, cast in England, is the largest in New England. Concerts by famous carillonneurs from all over the world are given Sundays at 6:00 P.M. from late June through August. Hearing a concert is a delightful way to spend a summer evening, perhaps also picnicking on the green lawn of Cohasset Common. Call (617) 383–1083 for a schedule.

A hop, skip, and a jump from Cohasset Common is a really nice take-out restaurant, Strawberry Parfait, at 2 Pleasant Street (617–383–9681). A green lawn with flower gardens holds a scattering of picnic tables, where you can take your fried clams, burgers, lobster rolls, and ice cream. Around the corner is an excellent local gallery, the South Shore Art Center, at 119 Ripley Road (617–383–9548), featuring the work of local artists. Founded in 1955, the South Shore Art Center sponsors the longest continuously operating art festival in the country each summer on Cohasset Common.

When you drive through downtown Scituate, you may be startled to see a fifteenth-century-Roman-style tower standing in the middle of a green near the library. It's the **Lawson Tower,** built at huge expense by Thomas Lawson, "the Copper King" of Wall Street. Lawson made a fortune in copper, only to be ruined in later life. The water tower stood on his large estate here, called Dreamwold, complete with its own railroad and post office. He wanted to cloak the tower's utilitarian purpose. Today, Dreamwold is condos; however, in 1902 Lawson gave the water tower to the town and it now plays carillon concerts in summer. At 153 feet tall, the tower is a landmark for ships at sea and offers a clear vista of the South Shore when you climb its steps. To see the tower, take a left off Route 3A south onto First Parish Road and drive up behind the First Parish Church. The tower is opened for tours during the summer and in December by the Scituate Historical Society (617–545–1083 or 617–545–0474), as are several other sites.

One is the 1811 granite **Scituate Lighthouse,** out on Lighthouse Point at the corner of Lighthouse and Rebecca roads. In the War of 1812, the keeper's quick-witted teenage daughters prevented the British from sacking the town. Seeing two barges approach in the harbor, they grabbed up a fife and drum and played with all their might, hiding behind some cedars. The British, thinking an entire regiment awaited, beat a hasty retreat. For this feat, the girls went down in history as "the Army of Two."

Front Street in Scituate bustles with interesting little shops, galleries, and restaurants and a working fishing fleet anchors at its northern end. At the Quarterdeck, at 206 Front Street, you'll find a blend of wares so eclectic that they also caught the eye of Hollywood scouts choosing locations for *The Witches of Eastwick.* This little shop with windows on Scituate Harbor is crammed with antiques, imports, nautical items, and an impressive collection of historic postcards of local scenes.

Handy to Front Street is the Allen House Bed & Breakfast, a large white Victorian high on a hill overlooking the harbor. The house is nicely fitted out with richly patterned wallpapers and fabrics conveying an antique sensibility. Unusual antiques grace the dining room, large guest parlor, and four guest rooms, several with ocean views and two with private baths. Stupendous four-course breakfasts start off with coffee and juices, or mulled cider or hot cranberry cup in cold weather. Next a fruit plate, which might be strawberries in port wine with whipped cream, pineapple boats with ginger-honey cream, or warm berry compote with *crème fraîche.* Entrees range from mushrooms in a tarragon cream sherry sauce with toast points to plum crisp with pecan topping. The meal ends with homemade muffins, popovers, and scones, or perhaps an apricot lattice tart. If this doesn't fortify you enough, innkeepers Christine and Iain Gilmour enjoy serving a proper British cuppa in the afternoon, with cream and scones. Write the Gilmours at 18 Allen Place, Scituate 02066, or call (617) 545–8221 (doubles, $79–$109).

The stretch of Route 3A between Scituate and Marshfield is one of the prettiest drives on the South Shore. The tidal marshes of the North River reach out for miles on both sides. The play of sunlight is an artist's dream and makes this road a joy to drive. In a reverse scenario of pristine wilderness to industrial wasteland, the river's banks once shouldered dozens of shipyards and factories, now gone. More than a thousand ships were built here, including the brig *Beaver,* of Boston Tea Party fame, and the ship *Columbia,* the first to carry the Stars and Stripes around the world.

Just over the little bridge at the town line of Marshfield, you'll see Mary's Boat Livery (617–837–2322) on the right. You can rent a boat here for either a half-day or all day and take it up the North River, an ideal way to see its scenic meanderings.

In its day, the 1699 **Winslow House** was a mansion, as befit its owner, Judge Isaac Winslow, grandson of Plymouth Colony Governor Edward Winslow, the Pilgrim founder of Marshfield. The leading men of Plymouth Colony were entertained here, at formal teas and dinners. Although the house looks plain by our standards, its Jacobean staircase with acorn finials was a standout. Behind the Georgian paneling in the drawing room is a secret chamber where Tories reportedly hid. Daniel Webster had an estate in Marshfield for twenty years, and his law office was moved here; the office has letters and photos of Webster's. Also on the property are a blacksmith shop and a one-room schoolhouse. The Winslow House is open from 1:00 to 5:00 P.M. Wednesday through Sunday, mid-June through mid-October. Admission is $2.00 for adults and 50 cents for children. Call (617) 837–5753. The house is at the corner of Webster and Careswell streets.

No matter what the season, it always smells like Thanksgiving at Gerard Farm, a family business for fifty years. The smells of roasting turkey and chicken fill the air at this wonderful shop that sells many kinds of homemade foods, with freshly-roasted turkey its specialty. Where else can you get a thick turkey sandwich made with two kinds of bread, cranberry sauce, stuffing, and mayonnaise? Freezers stock frozen turkey pies ("all dark meat" and "all white meat"), turkey croquettes, roast turkeys, and turkey soup. The shop is at 1331 Ocean Street (Route 139). Call (617) 834–7682.

Each spring thousands of herring fight their way upstream in the North River to spawn in ponds, as they have for centuries. The herring, also called alewives, were a vital source of food for the Pilgrims and the Indians. Colonists regulated fishing rights strictly, appointing a "herring superintendent" to oversee the harvesting and distribution of fish. Widows, spinsters, and other needy persons were given bushel baskets of fish. There are a half-dozen points on the South Shore where you can watch the herring run. A good spot is **Herring Run Park** on Route 14 in Pembroke, which celebrates the herring run with an annual fish fry in late April. The herring are dipped from the brook with nets. A modern-day herring superintendent oversees the action and unsuccessfully tries to dissuade children from wading in. The fish are fried in big cast-iron skillets over an open grill and served with cornbread and baked beans. (The squeamish can eat hot dogs.) For the date and other information, call the Plymouth County Development Council at (617) 826–3136.

Pilgrim and Cranberry Country

The town of Duxbury was settled as early as 1625, by Pilgrims from the nearby Plymouth Colony. Among them were names that ring through history: Alden, Standish, Brewster. After John Alden won his wife, Priscilla, away from Myles Standish, they lived out their later years in a tiny house built in 1653. The **John Alden House** is cramped and dark and looks none too comfortable. Its low, rough plaster ceilings were made of crushed clam and oyster shells, and even the formal parlor has a stark look to it. Other features of the house are the cambered panels in the "best room," and the gunstock beams in the bed chambers. The house, located at 105 Alden Street, off Route 3A, is open from 10:00 A.M. to 5:00 P.M. daily except Monday, from late June until Labor Day. Admission is $1.00 for adults and 50 cents for children. Call (617) 934–6001 for information.

Down the street from the Alden House is a much brighter, contemporary place: the **Art Complex Museum.** This small but intriguing museum was founded by Carl Weyerhaeuser— grandson of the founder of the lumber company of the same name—and his wife, Edith, as a home for their private collection. Much of it is Asian art, as well as Shaker and American works. There are semiannual showings of contemporary New England artists. A unique feature of the museum is an authentic Japanese teahouse designed in Kyoto; authentic and traditional Japanese tea ceremonies are demonstrated on the last Sunday of the summer months. The museum, open from 1:00 to 4:00 P.M. Wednesday through Sunday, is at 189 Alden Street. Call (617) 934–6634.

When appetite calls, head for the home-style Milepost Tavern Restaurant (617–934–6801) on Route 3A. It's hard to explain how such an unadorned place can be so appealing, but there you are. Big factors are the friendly waitresses and good food. Besides homemade hearty soups and sandwiches, lunch specialties include baskets of fried clams and scallops or honey-dipped fried chicken, served with french fries. At dinner, you can choose from such standard, comforting offerings as chicken, veal, beef, and seafood, plus blackboard specials.

For dessert (or a luxurious breakfast), you can't beat **French Memories Bakery.** This bakery was founded by real French natives, who bake real French croissants and baguettes on the premises. They also create mouth-watering pastries that are colorful works of art: kiwi, strawberry, and apple tarts; chocolate mousse; brioches; and opera cake. The shop is at 459 Washington Street, next to Sweetser's General Store; call (617) 934–9020.

The town of Duxbury once had sixteen shipbuilders. The wealthiest of them, Ezra Weston and his son, Ezra Weston II, grew so rich that they both came to be called "King Caesar." In 1808, the son built a gorgeous, Federal-style mansion overlooking his wharves. The light-filled **King Caesar House** shows off exquisite woodwork and fanlight windows, as well as sweeping ocean views. One room displays treasures of the China Trade, such as Chinese writing implements and beautifully hand-painted fans. The two front parlors display rare French mural wallpapers. The many fine furnishings include a thirteen-light cabinet symbolic of the thirteen colonies, a 1795 girandole mirror, and Sandwich and cable glass (cable glass was made in a cable-shaped pattern to commemorate the laying of the first transatlantic cable from France to Duxbury, in 1869). The house, on King Caesar Road, is open from 1:00 to 4:00 P.M. on Tuesday through Sunday from early June through Labor Day and on Friday and Saturday in September. Admission is $3.00 for adults and 50 cents for children. Call (617) 934–6106.

If you follow King Caesar Road out to Duxbury Beach, you'll pass over the Powder Point Bridge, the longest wooden bridge on the eastern seaboard, some say the longest in the nation. About 2,200 feet long, it was first built in 1892 and was then rebuilt after it burned in 1985. Cars are welcome to cross this wide span, which offers a pretty view of a little inlet just before Duxbury Beach. The bridge is favored by fishermen; the inlet, by sailboarders. Duxbury Beach is a grand beach of several miles that faces the open Atlantic. It's one of the few South Shore beaches open to the public.

NEW ENGLAND'S LARGEST BREAKFAST MENU trumpets the sign at **Persy's Place** in Kingston. Indeed, you might spend all morning perusing the offerings: sixteen egg dishes; twelve kinds of omelets, including lobster, *chourico,* and "build-your-own"; and almost everything else your breakfast fancy might desire, from asparagus to rainbow trout, from finnan haddie to S.O.S. (uh, chipped beef on toast). Persy's hews to Yankee traditions with fish cakes, corned beef hash, Boston baked beans, and grilled cornbread (outstanding). Four generations of the Heston family (the youngest is "growing as fast as she can") serve breakfast all day long. The small dining rooms with wooden booths are so homey that they feel like your living room. An outdoor deck opens in nice weather. Next door, the owners run a small country store that sells hand-painted wooden decorations and the like. Persy's Place is at 117 Main Street (Route 3A), just south of exit 9 from Route 3. Call (617) 585–5464.

So much "Pilgrimiana" is awash in Plymouth that the *Mayflower* couldn't possibly carry it all back to England. Busloads of people from all over the world come to see Plymouth Rock enshrined in its odd mausoleum, Plimoth Plantation, and the *Mayflower II*, flooding the waterfront and its schlocky shops and restaurants.

If you're on Pilgrim overload, head for the **Whale Discovery Center,** which opened in 1991 and is unique among museums in focusing solely on whales. Its imaginative and innovative exhibits include interactive video, computer games, and hands-on activities that children as well as adults will enjoy. Making a head-to-tail exploration of a whale, from its nose and eyes down to its flukes, exhibits emphasize whale behavior and ecological concerns. One wall of exhibits is framed by a life-size blue neon outline of a humpback. Test your lung capacity against a whale's, or fish for plastic "krill," just as a whale does with its baleen. You can imitate recorded whale songs, and see your voice pattern graphically compared with the whales' on a computer screen. A computer game illustrates how whales can be identified by tail markings. *Whales Go to Hollywood* presents film cuts from *Down to the Sea in Ships* and *Moby Dick, Pinocchio,* and *Star Trek IV.* A video puppet show in 3-D shows how people have thought about whales from the time of the ancient Greeks and Christopher Columbus, on up to "save the whales" proponents. The Whale Discovery Center is located on Howland Street; call (508) 747–0015. Tickets cost $4.50 for adults and $3.25 for children. Hours are 9:00 A.M. to 5:00 P.M. daily year-round, except in winter, when the center opens only on weekends.

Armed with your new knowledge of whales, you might find that now's the ideal time to go whale-watching. Step across the street to Town Wharf, where you'll find **Capt. John Boats,** which runs four-hour whale-watching cruises from April through October to Stellwagen Bank, the whales' feeding ground. These boats have a high success rate and have spotted, among other kinds of whales, finback, humpback, right, and minke. Cruises cost $20.00 for adults and $14.00 for children. Call (508) 746–2643 or (800) 242–AHOY in Massachusetts. Capt. John Boats also runs harbor tours, cruises to Provincetown, and deep-sea fishing charters.

Massachusetts grows more than half the country's cranberries right here on the South Shore. In the fall, the landscape blazes with bogs in crimson. Locals routinely see the **cranberry harvest** in progress as they drive the country roads of Plymouth, Carver, Middleborough, and Wareham. The harvest is big business and well promoted—bus tours arrive en masse. Still, watching the colorful harvest is a great way to spend a crisp, sunny fall day, and one that will prompt you to reach for the camera. The wet-harvesting method first floods bogs and then uses water reels like giant eggbeaters to loosen the berries from the vines so that they float to the surface. The huge sea of red berries contrasts vibrantly with the deep blue of the water. Enriching the tones of this picture, workers wearing yellow hip-waders corral the berries. Then a hose vacuums them up into a truck. Harvesting goes on from about Labor Day to late October or early November. You'll pass several bogs on Route 44 west through Plymouth, down Seven Hills Road, and out Federal Furnace Road. Or drive out Routes 106 or 58.

You might want to sample some cranberry wine on your tour. If so, turn into the Plymouth Colony Winery (508–747–3334), on Pinewood Road in Plymouth, a left off Route 44 west. Housed in an 1890 cranberry-screening house, the winery also makes blueberry, raspberry, peach, and grape wines.

To learn all there is to know about cranberries, stop into the Cranberry World Visitors Center on the waterfront in Plymouth, the country's only museum devoted to cranberries. Exhibits illustrate cranberry history and trace harvesting methods and tools, from antique wooden scoops on up to modern ways. The cranberry bouncer, designed years ago, is still used to test ripeness by how high berries bounce. The free museum, on Water Street, is open May 1 to November 30, from 9:30 A.M. to 5:00 P.M. daily. Call (508) 747–2350.

Another cranberry country stop not to be missed is the **Edaville Railroad** on Route 58 in South Carver (508–866–4526). Edaville was once a cranberry plantation owned by grower Ellis D. Atwood, whose initials went into the name. You can ride around the bogs on Atwood's vintage, open-air railroad cars and see the harvest in season. Children enjoy the petting zoo, carousel, miniature Model T car rides, and paddlewheel steamboat. There's also a museum of antique railroad cars, fire engines, and trucks. A splendid time to visit is during the Cranberry Festival and Fair, the last two weekends in September. Woodsmen's contests, handmade cranberry-themed quilts, and cranberry foods are fair highlights. Edaville Railroad opens for the season in May, when its hours are noon to 5:00 P.M. weekends. In summer, hours are 10:00 A.M. to 5:30 P.M. daily. After Labor Day, it's open 10:00 A.M. to 3:00 P.M. weekdays and 10:00 A.M. to 5:30 P.M. weekends. In November and December, there's a Christmas Festival with thousands of lights put up; hours are 4:00 to 9:00 P.M. weekdays and 2:00 to 9:00 P.M. weekends. Admission is $12.50 for adults and $7.50 for children.

Way out in the sticks among the cranberry bogs is one of the finest restaurants on the South Shore—the Crane Brook Tea Room. When Emperor-to-be Akihito visited Massachusetts, this is where he dined. In a former iron foundry and cranberry-screening house overlooking a tranquil pond, the restaurant has transformed its rustic origins into a place of elegance and graciousness. The darkly romantic, living-room-size foyer invites you to rest amid armchairs and a glowing wood stove. An exquisitely created menu changes daily, based on the freshest and best seasonal ingredients. Special appetizers might include escargots with sun-dried tomatoes, garlic, and goat cheese or country pâté with pistachios in a Cumberland sauce. For dinner entrees, you might choose from paupiettes of sole and lobster, New Zealand venison, or roast pork in an old-fashioned mustard sauce. Desserts are made to order. The Crane Brook Tea Room is on Tremont Street in South Carver; call (508) 866–3235. It's closed Monday and Tuesday.

There's a lot to see at the **Middleborough Historical Museum.** You might start with the collection of Tom Thumb memorabilia, collected from General and Mrs. Tom Thumb's Middleborough house, built to their miniature size. The pair, who toured with P. T. Barnum, received gifts from queens, emperors, and kings. Also among the memorabilia are Tom's pipe and smoking stand, along with miniature clothing. The museum also has eighteenth- and nineteenth-century museum houses, antique vehicles, a blacksmith shop, and many period vignettes, such as a country store, an old-time print shop, and a straw hat works. Nineteenth-century wedding gowns, antique children's toys, and Indian artifacts are exhibited as well. The museum is located on Jackson Street, off Route 105, behind the police station. Hours are from 1:00 to 4:00 P.M. Wednesday through Sunday in July, August, and the first two weekends in September. Admission is $2.00 for adults and $1.00 for students. Call (508) 947–1969.

Middleborough is just south of Bridgewater, thick with interesting stops. Route 18 north all the way to East Bridgewater is lined with antiques shops, small stores in old houses filled with an agreeable clutter of furniture and collectibles. Look particularly for Antiques at Forge Pond and for Ye Old Tyme Shoppe.

Where Route 18 meets Route 106 west, you'll find a post office that has stood its ground since 1861. The **Elmwood Post Office** was commissioned by Abraham Lincoln. The Elmwood section of Bridgewater was the birthplace of the shoe industry, and a tannery was built here as early as 1650. Lincoln ordered the post office so that the village could ship badly needed shoes to the Union Army. The post office stands in a small, white-columned building, taking up only a tiny corner for its ancient black window grille and old-fashioned metal mailboxes with brass combination dials. Behind the grille is an old slant-topped wooden desk, and hanging above the desk is a framed picture of Lincoln. The post office shares its floor space with an antiques shop. Postmaster

Elmwood Post Office

Sally Flagg Aldrich is a member of the fourth generation in her family to serve as postmaster.

Elmwood was once called Joppa, after the biblical city of Joppa. The **Joppa Grill** (508–378–3510), a vintage country restaurant that dates to 1926, honors that name. From its striped canvas awnings to the old wooden tables and winged booths, the restaurant is virtually unchanged. Faithful regulars flock here—as they have for decades—for all-homemade food at affordable prices and complimentary appetizers of Joppa sticks—fried dough sprinkled with brown and confectionery sugars. The strongly traditional lunch and dinner menus include grilled cheese sandwiches, lobster sandwiches, chef's salads, broiled ham steak, lamb chops, pork chops, fried clams, and fried chicken; deep-dish apple pie and grapenut pudding are featured for dessert. The Joppa Grill is on Route 18 north, 1 block up from where Route 106 bends east.

Last but not least on Route 18, look on the left in Whitman to find Peaceful Meadows Ice Cream (617–447–3889), which dispenses excellent homemade ice cream at the edge of a cow pasture and has picnic tables. Be sure to sit so that you can watch the cows in the peaceful meadows.

Another country restaurant in Hanson is an excellent place to go any time of day, for any reason: breakfast, coffee, dessert, snacks, lunch, dinner, you name it. At **Phil's Family Restaurant** (617–294–8147), truckers and construction workers—who have always known how to eat well and cheaply at the same time—perennially hunker down at the counter and the orange-and-blue Formica booths. Everything is homemade, from recipes contributed by family, friends, and customers. If you can't find something here you like, your mother didn't raise you right. Breakfast, served all day, ranges from steak and eggs to blueberry pancakes and "build-your-own" omelets. At lunch and dinner, there are forty kinds of sandwiches (counting burgers and hot dogs), plus dishes like meatloaf, chicken Parmesan, and liver and onions. The all-homemade desserts, numbering thirty-two, claim some originals as well as traditions: Betty's chocolate macaroon pie, French silk pie, apple crisp, and strawberry shortcake. The largesse extends to a bakery counter, selling enormous muffins, pies, cookies, and brownies. Phil's is located at 1357 Main Street (Route 27), west of Route 58.

Off the Beaten Path on Cape Cod and the Islands

1. Cape Cod Canal Cruises
2. Aptucxet Trading Post
3. Ashumet Holly Reservation and Wildlife Sanctuary
4. Cornelia Carey Sanctuary
5. Cahoon Museum of American Art
6. Green Briar Jam Kitchen and Nature Center
7. Sandy Neck
8. Cape Cod Scenic Railroad
9. Cape Cod Rail Trail
10. New England Fire and History Museum
11. Old Grist Mill
12. Old Atwood House
13. Brass band concerts
14. Crosswind Landing
15. Monomoy National Wildlife Refuge
16. Salt Pond Visitors Center of Cape Cod National Seashore
17. Art galleries
18. Just Dessert
19. Wintertime cruises
20. Race Point
21. Whale watching
22. Cedar Tree Neck
23. Takemmoy Farm
24. Menemsha
25. Gay Head Cliffs
26. Maria Mitchell Science Center and Birthplace
27. Nantucket Lifesaving Museum
28. Eel Point
29. Sconset

Cape Cod and the Islands

Although Cape Cod is the site of the most legendary summer traffic jams in the state of Massachusetts, there must be something here to see or there would be no lines.

Many sneer that overcrowding and tacky development have ruined the Cape. Untrue. Yes, whole towns have surrendered to strip malls, T-shirt shops, and fast-food and factory outlets. But pockets of untouched beauty endure: landscapes of windswept salt marshes and weathered houses, windmills and lighthouses, beach roses and dunes. A good 40 miles of coastline is preserved as the Cape Cod National Seashore, and its majestic beaches look just as wild now as they did years ago, when Henry David Thoreau, and, later, Eugene O'Neill walked the sands. And the Cape's northern, bay side still harbors serene villages of sea captains' houses.

Shaped like a giant arm, Cape Cod juts into the Atlantic Ocean, with Bourne at its "shoulder," Chatham at the "elbow," and Provincetown way out at the "fist," the northeast tip. The landscape gets wilder as you head out toward the very end, the place of fabled hundred-foot dunes, wide-open beaches, and acres of waving grasses. For some reason, the shoulder is known as the Upper Cape and the tip as the Lower Cape (also the Outer Cape). In between is the commercialized Mid-Cape.

The Cape's two island neighbors, Martha's Vineyard and Nantucket, are distinctly different, despite their common whaling heritage. Martha's Vineyard is much larger, and it has a more varied terrain. Diminutive Nantucket is less tourist-ized and is a wilder place of rolling moors.

The Cape and Islands are lovelier in the off-season. The summertime hordes trammel almost every acre of the Cape and disgorge from ferries and cruise ships onto the Islands. Though fall and spring are no longer quite the secret they were, they're much more tranquil times to visit. The surge of tourism dies down to a low roar, and the natives regain friendlier selves, bolstered by resuming their small-town rhythms.

For travel information, contact the Cape Cod Chamber of Commerce, P.O. Box 1001, Hyannis 02664-1001; (508) 362–3225.

Upper Cape

Before you even get to the Cape, there are things to see. Most people don't give the Cape Cod Canal a second thought, except for how fast they can get over the bridges in heavy traffic. But those two graceful steel bridges, the Sagamore Bridge and the Bourne Bridge, won a national award for "most beautiful steel bridges" when they were completed in 1935. From them, you can see for miles over the Upper Cape and watch the sun cascading across the 500-foot-wide expanse, the widest sea-level canal in the world. There is a constant parade of boats in the canal; some 20,000 ships a year pass through it, making it one of the world's busiest canals. Myles Standish first suggested a canal here in 1623, but it took until 1914 to get the 17-mile-long route built. The U.S. Army Corps of Engineers oversees the canal and maintains a popular visitor center in Buzzards Bay. But few people stop into the reception area at the administration building just down the road (508–759–4431).

The white wooden building sits hard by the banks of the canal, dwarfed by the towering legs of the Bourne Bridge. Two red-and-yellow tugs ride at anchor nearby. In the marine traffic controller's office, you can see a large diorama of the canal and watch the controller at work behind a massive bank of computer monitors, radios, and closed-circuit television screens. You'll hear the crackling broadcasts of approaching ships too. A slide show explains how the traffic control system works. The visitor reception area is open from 9:00 A.M. to 4:00 P.M. weekdays. From the Sagamore rotary, follow signs for Buzzards Bay to Main Street. Turn left at the first set of traffic lights onto Academy Drive.

The Corps also sponsors such programs in the canal area as nature walks, bike trips, and camp fire programs. Two 8-mile service roads paralleling the canal are nice, flat terrain for bicycling and offer views unseen by drivers. The roads are accessible from more than a half-dozen points on the mainland and on the Cape. Mainland parking spots include behind the Friendly Ice Cream Shop off the Sagamore Bridge rotary, at Herring Run on Route 6 between the rotary and Buzzards Bay, and at Scusset Beach. You might bike out to Scusset Beach, a long, sandy beach with bathhouses and a snack stand, for the afternoon. On the Cape side, you can park at Freezer Road at Sandwich Marina or at Monument Beach–Pocasset (east from the Bourne Bridge rotary; turn left at the sign).

If you'd like an even better view of the canal, take a narrated sight-seeing cruise along it, perhaps by moonlight or sunset or accompanied by some rousing jazz music. **Cape Cod Canal Cruises** (508–295–3883) runs two- and three-hour daily cruises from Onset Bay, spring through fall. Steaming along on a 200-passenger boat with an observation deck, you'll see such historic places as the site of President Grover Cleveland's summer mansion, Gray Gables.

By taking the Bourne Bridge over the canal and onto Route 28, you can make a loop tour of the Cape's chunky shoulder. The first stop is Bourne, where there is a jewel of a little museum, the **Aptucxet Trading Post.** This primitive-looking building is a replica of the first trading post in English-speaking North America, which stood here in 1627 and was built by the Pilgrims for trade with the Dutch and Indians. But it looks and is authentic in many ways. The inside is fitted out with wooden barrels of tobacco, furs hanging on the wall, and wooden scales. Here it's easy to picture Pilgrims and Indians trading together. Traders used wampum, bits of shells that were America's first form of currency. Some architectural details are seventeenth century, such as beams, wide-planked flooring, and leaded-glass diamond-pane windows.

Glass cases hold seventeenth-century potsherds, Indian arrowheads, and stone tools and wampum found on the site. Also on the grounds are President Cleveland's Victorian summer railroad station for arriving guests and a replica of an eighteenth-century saltworks with rolling roofs. There are picnic tables on the wooded grounds. The post is open daily except Monday from May through Columbus Day, 10:00 A.M. to 5:00 P.M. weekdays and 2:00 to 5:00 P.M. Sundays. Admission is $1.50 for adults and 50 cents for children. Call (508) 759–9487. To get to the museum, turn right just after the Bourne Bridge and go 1 mile to a cemetery on the left; then turn right under a white railroad underpass onto Aptucxet Road, which jogs right. A windmill stands at the entrance.

Continuing south on Route 28, turn left onto Route 151 in Falmouth. Just off 151, you'll find a wildlife sanctuary that's full of Christmas spirit year-round—the **Ashumet Holly Reservation and Wildlife Sanctuary.** Here grows the largest native holly collection in New England—eight species and sixty-five varieties. They're all identified along a nature trail surrounding a grassy pond. A walk here is a wonderful discovery of holly's endless variety beyond the familiar red berry. Some hollies are trees, towering 20 or 30 feet tall; others bear orange or black berries. Berries turn color in late October, lingering through March unless robins and squirrels eat them all. Fragrant wreaths and swags of greenery are sold at Christmastime. A barn swallow colony nests in the barn May through August. The sanctuary, at 286 Ashumet Road in East Falmouth (508–563–6390), is open from dawn to dusk. Trail fees are $3.00 for adults and $2.00 for seniors and children.

Some people never gave up on the alternative-energy push of the 1970s. You'll meet a few of their numbers at the New Alchemy Institute, a twelve-acre working research farm. Projects include energy-efficient housing, landscape design, and organic gardening. You can wander vegetable, herb, and flower gardens and can tour composting, solar, and geodesic greenhouses. A "superinsulated" auditorium made out of a drafty old dairy barn is so well built that it needs only body heat and the warmth of lights and appliances to warm it. A farm stand sells some of the excellent produce, and a visitor center has exhibits on what you can do to save energy, offers garden supplies for sale, and runs a slide show depicting the farm through the seasons. The institute is at 237 Hatchville Road, off Route 151 in East Falmouth (508–564–6301). Self-guided tours can be taken from 10:00 A.M. to 4:00 P.M. daily; guided tours, costing $2.00 (free for children) are given at 1:00 P.M. on Saturday and more often than that during summer.

Down at the end of Scranton Avenue in Falmouth is a Mobil-rated four-star restaurant, The Regatta (508–548–5400), in a beautiful waterfront setting on the harbor. Its specialties are regional American, French, and international cuisine.

Before you get to Woods Hole, off Route 28 and via a right turn onto Quisset Harbor Road is a lovely little sanctuary, the **Cornelia Carey Sanctuary** (locals call it "the Knob"). The road winds around picturesque Quisset Harbor with its fishing boats and comes to a dead end. Where a sign announces

PRIVATE ROAD, there's a fence in front of a large house with a turnstile. Walk through the turnstile and over a stone-fortified causeway. A small wooded area of red cedar and oak opens up to a bare, grassy promontory high up, offering views of Buzzards Bay and the Elizabeth Islands. The Salt Pond Areas Bird Sanctuaries owns the land; call (508) 548–0711 for information.

Immediately after Route 28 passes Route 130 heading east in Cotuit, you'll see a red colonial building on the left, the **Cahoon Museum of American Art.** The setting of this small but gemlike museum heightens the flavor of its engaging collections. Once a tavern and stagecoach stop, the house was built in 1775. The six galleries have original low plaster ceilings, wide-planked floors, nineteenth-century stenciled walls and floorboards, and period wooden furniture. These serenely antique surroundings give the feeling that the paintings hang in a private home. Primitive artists Ralph and Martha Cahoon bought the house for their studio in the 1940s. The museum opened in 1984, with the Cahoons' paintings as the heart of the permanent collections. Ralph was fond of painting mermaids, posing them whimsically in Cape settings of ocean, lighthouses, and ships. These paintings just have to bring a smile to your face, as you see mermaids cavorting in hot-air balloons shaped like fish and birds, or doing their laundry using a whale for a washboard. Also on exhibit are some of the largest and most gorgeous sailors' Valentines I've ever seen, set in gold-framed, octagonal shadowboxes. These beautiful pieces, traditionally bought by sailors for their wives and sweethearts in the West Indies, were made of hundreds of tiny pink, white, and purple seashells formed into patterns of flowers and other elaborate designs. The collection also includes the work of primitive itinerant portrait painters, marine artists, Hudson River landscape artists, and American impressionist painters. The museum is open from 10:00 A.M. to 4:00 P.M. Wednesday through Saturday and from 1:00 to 4:00 P.M. Sunday (closed from January to March). Call (508) 428–7581. Admission is free.

When you come out of the museum, drive down Main Street in Cotuit, opposite the museum. This is one of the loveliest and most unspoiled Main Streets on the Cape. It slopes gently 3½ miles down to the sea, passing tidy shingled and clapboarded houses with well-built wooden fences and tall, stately trees. There are almost no commercial establishments, save for the ancient Cotuit Grocery, a gas station, and a couple of antiques shops. You'll pass the 1846 Old Meeting House, now the Mariners' Lodge, and a small library. Main Street winds through salt marshes and sheltered inlets, dead-ending at an intimate town beach.

Leaving Cotuit, take Route 130 north to the town of Sandwich. This attractive, colonial-looking village is famous for its Sandwich Glass Museum, among other attractions. Less known is the **Green Briar Jam Kitchen and Nature Center,** where they still make jam the way they have since 1903. If you tour the kitchen, you'll feel like you've stepped into your grandmother's kitchen. Copper counters line the blue-and-white expanse, and sunny windows brim with pink geraniums. A many-burnered, 1920 cast-iron gas stove runs the length of the kitchen, flanked by a Hoosier cabinet and big wooden barrels of sugar. During a jammaking class, steam rises in your face, releasing the delicious warm fruit smells. The classes are given year-round. A gift shop sells more than a hundred kinds of homemade jams, jellies, and preserves, from popular strawberry, raspberry, and blueberry to beach-plum jellies and marmalades. In the fall and winter, the kitchen makes cranberry conserve, tomato relish, and mincemeat.

A local Sandwich woman, Ida Putnam, started the Green Briar Jam Kitchen, using many recipes from her friend Fannie Merritt Farmer's famous cookbook. Naturalist and author Thornton Burgess roamed the jam kitchen's woods as a boy, later basing his Old Briar Patch and Smiling Pool on spots in those woods. The Green Briar Jam Kitchen and Nature Center, at 6 Discovery Hill Road in East Sandwich, gives daily tours May to December; call (508) 888–6870.

Sandwich doesn't have many restaurants, but there are a couple of good ones. The casual Sandwich's Sandwiches, at Russell's Corner (508–888–1221), is mostly for takeout, since it has only three wooden barrels for tables. You build your own sandwich, choosing from extensive lists of ingredients. The Daniel Webster Inn, at 149 Main Street (508–888–3622), is a cozily colonial place that serves hearty meats and seafoods.

Mid-Cape

A spectacular barrier beach called **Sandy Neck** stretches over the town line between Sandwich and Barnstable. Calmer than the pounding surf of the National Seashore, this beach is backed by lots of dunes and beach grasses. Hiking trails wind through the dunes. Alas, the days of walking on dunes are virtually gone; fragile dunes easily erode underfoot, and if you walk on the dunes, you'll be asked to leave. But you can't hurt the view. To reach Sandy Neck, turn left on Sandy Neck Road off Route 6A. It costs $8.00 to park in the small parking lot, which fills up rapidly on weekends, holidays, and hot days. For information, call the gate house at (508) 362–8300. If you'd like a view of the splendid Great Marshes on Sandy Neck's south side, drive a little farther east on Route 6A and turn left onto either Bone Hill Road or Millway in Barnstable.

Just off Route 6A on Route 149 in the center of Barnstable Village is a store that's more museum than store—the Barnstable Stove Shop (508–362–9913). Rusting hulks of stoves line the drive up to the weathered old barn that serves as showroom. Proudly gleaming with the shiny new faces given them by owner Doug Pacheco stand several dozen antique cast-iron stoves. The potbellied stoves, parlor stoves, and sturdy kitchen ranges are so beautifully restored that they look brand-new. A Glenwood parlor stove bears intricate scrollwork over almost every square inch and sports a 1-foot-tall fancy chrome finial. Hundreds more are in storage or under repair. The store is closed Wednesday and Sunday.

As you travel east on the Cape, it's much more fun and scenic to take the windier Route 6A—the Cranberry Highway—than to go barreling along Route 6—the Mid-Cape Highway, which reveals almost nothing along the way. Route 6A passes right through the main streets of three attractive northside villages: Barnstable, Yarmouthport, and Brewster, lined with old sea captains' houses, general stores, and inns and restaurants. You might particularly poke about the antiques shops in Barnstable Village, taking time to stop into the Trayser Memorial Museum of local history, located in the handsome old brick custom house.

By the time you get to Hyannis, you've hit some of the

worst the Cape has to offer. Lots of commercialism and strip malls densely pack this area. Still, it's the departure point for the **Cape Cod Scenic Railroad.** Rolling along in refurbished 1930s coaches provides a luxurious and leisurely view of the Cape's northside scenery on the way to Sagamore, some of which scenery can't be seen from the road. Along the way, you'll gaze out on farmland, cranberry bogs, salt marshes, dunes, and the village of Sandwich. If the time is right, you can watch the sunset over the canal. The dinner train serves up a five-course meal just as it did years ago, with white linen service and fresh flowers. The restored turn-of-the-century parlor car is appointed with mahogany tables, leaded glass, and brass fixtures.

The dinner train costs $42.50 per person. Fares for the scenic train ride are $10.50 for adults, $6.50 for children, and $9.50 for senior citizens. Trains run on weekends in spring, fall, and winter, and daily except Monday in summer. Call ahead for departure times and reservations: (508) 771–3788.

Just east of Hyannis lies a tiny and little-known village called Craigville, a secluded religious community. Like Oak Bluffs on Martha's Vineyard, this community grew out of summertime evangelist meetings held in tents surrounding a tabernacle. Small cottages began to replace the tents around 1873. The quaint, narrow village streets with their 15-mile-per-hour speed limit wind from cottage to cottage, where people of all faiths now live. The white tabernacle still stands and holds summertime ecumenical Sunday services, with its wooden doors opened out in the spirit of an open-air tabernacle. This is a continuing religious community, and there are lots of children about. But if visitors drive slowly and discreetly, they are welcome on the private roads. Nearby are Craigville Beach and the Craigville Conference Center. To get to Craigville village, take Route 28 to the Centerville traffic lights, where a sign points you to Centerville and the Craigville Conference Center and Beach. Turn left, and follow that road to the village.

Tucked into a bend of Route 6A in Yarmouthport is one of the Cape's top restaurants, the Cranberry Moose. Housed in an attractive, circa-1755 cranberry-colored cape with a massive trumpet vine climbing its walls, the Cranberry Moose has airy, contemporary dining rooms with light woods and white linen service. It offers innovative American dishes and has a changing menu; examples are fresh native seafoods and meats. Call ahead for weekend dinner reservations (508–362–3501). The Cranberry Moose is at 43 Main Street.

By way of contrast, Jack's Outback Restaurant, at 161 Hallet Street in Yarmouthport (508–362–6690), has none of your traditional restaurant amenities such as menus or service. You have to write up your own order, get your own coffee and silverware, and bus your own table. Offerings of the day are handwritten on a corkboard. When you walk in, you'll see a blue counter with stools; it overlooks the open kitchen, where most days you can see Jack at the griddle—he's the one with frazzled gray hair and a checked flannel shirt. His expertly cooked breakfasts include bacon and eggs, toast, and Belgian waffles. Lunches run to sandwiches and salads, including macaroni salad; quiches; and homemade soups. Besides breakfast and lunch, Jack's Outback serves diner-style dinners, such as roast beef and potatoes and New England boiled dinner. Open daily.

To get there, look for a store called Design Works in a small complex of shops on Route 6A east. Turn right into the driveway next to it and drive around behind the shops, where you'll see a gray-and-white building.

Any biking enthusiasts should definitely try their wheels on the **Cape Cod Rail Trail** bike path, a 20-mile stretch from Dennis to Eastham that follows the old right of way of the Penn Central Railroad. The easy, flat terrain passes some lovely scenery: stands of cedar and scrub pine, horse farms, cranberry bogs, salt marshes, beaches, and kettle ponds. Despite the Rail Trail's popularity, this is still one of the great things to do on the Cape. One of the nicest things about the Rail Trail is that you can use it to bike to the beaches along the way, thereby escaping the parking aggravations.

You can join the trail almost anywhere you like and can bike for as long as you want. Access is from more than a dozen points, clearly marked by signs on Routes 6 and 6A. The southerly trailhead is at a parking lot on Route 134, just south of Route 6 in South Dennis; the northern end comes out at the Salt Pond Visitors Center of the Cape Cod National Seashore. There are plenty of take-out stands, ice-cream shops, rest rooms, and bike-rental shops along the way. For information about the Rail Trail, call Nickerson State Park at (508) 896–3491. A good trail guide is *The Cape Cod Bike Book,* by William E. Peace ($2.50), available at the Salt Pond Visitors Center and many Cape bookshops.

The town of Brewster has several museums spread out along Route 6A, the most intriguing among them being the **New England Fire and History Museum** (508–896–5711). This museum is a collection of small-town buildings set around a little green, with a children's play area in the middle. You'll find a big barn, a blacksmith shop, the Union Fire Company (once under the direction of Benjamin Franklin), and an 1890 apothecary shop. The barn houses early hand-pulled and horse-drawn fire engines, with huge spoked wheels, leather buckets, and handsome brass bells and lanterns. A lighted diorama re-creates the famous 1871 Chicago fire, complete with clanging bells and smoke. Downstairs is the world's only 1929 Mercedes-Benz fire engine, as well as a collection of fire hats donated by the late Arthur Fiedler, who loved fire trucks. Hours are 10:00 A.M. to 4:00 P.M. weekdays and noon to 4:00 P.M. from mid-May through mid-September and only on weekends through Columbus Day. Tickets cost $4.00.

Another family-oriented Brewster stop is the Bassett Wild Animal Farm (508–896–3224), a rustic sort of combination small-zoo-and-farm. It's especially fun in the spring for children to see the new baby animals, which might include fox kits, goat kids, and chicks and geese. The white-tailed deer are so tame that they wag their tails like dogs when you approach with food pellets. In a large fenced area, you can mingle freely with the ducks, sheep, goats, pigs, and rabbits. You'll also meet a crow named Irving that says "Oh, boy!" There are more unusual animals too: a ring-tailed lemur from Madagascar, zebu cattle from India, and a South American green-wing macaw. In the pastures out back are pony rides and hayrides, and there are picnic tables in the shade. The animal farm is on Tubman Road, marked by a green sign on Route 137. Admission is $4.75 for adults and $3.75 for children. Hours are 10:00 A.M. to 5:00 P.M. daily, mid-May through mid-September.

Brewster is also where you'll find Chillingsworth, the best

restaurant on the Cape. It has won a national reputation for itself—four stars from the *Mobil Guide*—and is ranked with the best in the United States. The rambling, 300-year-old white house was built by a passenger on the *Mayflower.* Its five dining rooms are intimate and elegant, with eighteenth-century French furniture, working fireplaces, Empire paintings, and a large collection of cookbooks. The seven-course French dinner is served amid candlelight, white linen, antique china, fresh flowers, and crystal. A more casual lunch/brunch in summer is served in a flower-filled greenhouse. Dinner reservations are essential; there are two seatings. Call (508) 896–3640. Chillingsworth is right on Main Street (Route 6A). It closes after Thanksgiving and reopens before Memorial Day.

Chatham juts out at the Cape's elbow and so is almost surrounded by water, giving it some of the most spectacular views and nicest beaches on the entire Cape. To admire the view, drive out Shore Road along the ocean's edge, winding up at the Chatham Lighthouse.

There's so much in Chatham that you could spend a week here and not do everything. Of the half-dozen historic landmarks, one qualifies as a family affair. In the nineteenth century, the **Old Grist Mill** belonged to curator Everett Eldredge's grandfather. With a personal stake in the mill, Eldredge is proud to show off its history. The eight-sided mill was built in 1797 with a huge, horse-drawn drive shaft to turn the sails to catch the wind. In a strong wind, the mill could grind a bag of corn in ten minutes; other times, it might take all day. Going to the mill used to be a social break for farmers, who fed the meal to farm animals or made it into brown bread and Indian pudding. Today the mill's cool, dim interior is quiet and holds only some historic photographs. You can feel the roughness of its massive wooden beams and admire the heft of its solid lower millstone. Upstairs, you can see the huge upper grindstone. The Old Grist Mill is on Shattuck Place. It's open daily except Tuesdays in the summer from 9:00 A.M. to 4:00 P.M., or whenever Eldredge feels like closing.

A treasure trove for learning about Chatham's history is tucked away in a solitary wood-framed house, the **Old Atwood House.** Five generations of a sea captain's family lived here, from about 1752. Nineteenth-century pieces and memorabilia fill the fireplaced kitchen, parlor, borning room, keeping room, and music room. A whole gallery is full of portraits of Chatham sea captains. Among those persons were Captain Isaac White, who made a record, 120-day, New York-to-Shanghai run on his clipper ship *Independent,* and Captain Oliver Eldredge, hired as a cook for eight men at the age of nine.

Black-and-white photographs show historic local scenes: the railroad depot, the coastline, and Twin Lights. There are lots of maritime artifacts too, such as a bottle of real whale oil. One room showcases hundreds of seashells on glass shelves, shining pink and white in the sunlight. Another room is devoted to noted Cape Cod author Joseph C. Lincoln. A barn in back displays the realistic murals of Alice Stallknecht Wight, each portraying Chatham townspeople and religious themes, such as Christ preaching from a dory. All this costs only $3.00 admission ($1.00 for students). The Old Atwood House is located at 347 Stage Harbor Road, about ¾ mile from the rotary at the Congregational church on Route 28. The museum is open from 2:00 to 5:00 P.M. Monday, Wednesday, and Friday, June 11 to September 28.

Every summer Friday night, **brass band concerts** unfold in Kate Gould Park on Main Street, a decades-long tradition whose pleasure is undimmed by the thousands who come. People spread out on blankets and lawn chairs and bring their babies, dogs, popcorn, and coolers. Lights dramatize the gleaming white bandstand and snapping red uniforms. Energetic, octogenarian bandleader Whit Tileston, who has wielded his baton for more than forty years, shows no signs of tiring. Tileston leads the band in old favorites, inviting the audience to sing along, do the bunnyhop, and waltz; he also keeps track of lost teddy bears for the children. These evenings take on a magical quality as dusk falls, with floating clouds of brightly colored balloons and children waving glow-in-the-dark light sticks.

Shops and restaurants thickly line Chatham's Main Street. A local dining favorite is Christian's, at 443 Main Street (508–945–3362). Its Upstairs at Christian's serves a lighter and less expensive menu in a darkly masculine, clubby piano bar set with wing chairs, sofas, and books. An outdoor deck overlooks the action on Main Street. The surprisingly long and imaginative menu includes appetizers of cheese and onion quesadilla and deep-fried raviolis; pizzas; and lots of seafood and pasta specialties, such as cod cakes, mussels, pan-fried spaghettini, and *lasagna al forno.*

For a more whimsical dining experience, you can't beat **Crosswind Landing** at the Chatham Municipal Airport (508–945–5955), where gourmet breakfast and lunch food is served (you'll never eat this well at Boston's Logan Airport). The upstairs dining room overlooks the runway, a tiny outpost of an airstrip. The buzzings of light planes counterpoint your meal. The small and intimate dining room is dominated by a lighthearted mural of aviation history, complete with a wing-walker on a biplane. Pink tablecoths topped with glass show off such diner-contributed collages as pictures of dogs or babies and headlines from the *National Enquirer.* A sunny outdoor deck overlooks both the runway and a kids' play area, which contains a mock wooden airplane (the *Spruce Coot*) and a rowboat. The scrumptious food ranges from homemade pastries and waffles, such as strawberry-rhubarb crumb cake with fresh whipped cream, to homemade soups and chowders, sandwiches, quesadillas, and blue-plate specials like chicken pie. The restaurant is open from May to Columbus Day.

The screen door slams often with the many arrivals at Marion's Pie Shop on the west side of town, at 2022 Main Street (508–432–9439). Everything is made from scratch. Irresistible smells emanate from freshly baked cinnamon rolls and hand-cut doughnuts, cranberry nut and zucchini-pineapple breads, and old-fashioned two-crust pies such as apple, peach, and blueberry. Chicken and clam pies make great take-home dinners.

At the very tip of Chatham, past the lighthouse, you'll find **Monomoy National Wildlife Refuge,** on Morris Island (508–945–0594). Its two barrier islands, North Monomoy Island and South Monomoy Island, were once a single 7-mile-long island that was split in two by the blizzard of 1978. These starkly beautiful islands are splendid spots for birding and hiking. Their wild, windswept terrain includes tidal flats and salt marshes, thickets and dunes, and inspiring ocean vistas from every angle. The sea winds will clear your brain cells thoroughly of any city anxieties. Thousands of birds use the islands as a staging area, and close to 300 species have been spotted here. The many shorebirds include marbled godwits, piping plovers, oystercatchers, whimbrels, and terns.

The only access to Monomoy is by private boat or guided tour. Two groups lead day trips: the Wellfleet Bay Wildlife Sanctuary (508–349–2615) and the Cape Cod Museum of Natural History (508–896–3867). Wellfleet Bay offers half-day or all-day trips year-round, most frequently in summer, ranging in price from $30 to $45. To get a current list of trip dates and prices, write Wellfleet Bay Wildlife Sanctuary, P.O. Box 236, South Wellfleet, 02663. The Cape Cod Museum of Natural History runs trips May through October ($35 and $68). A special overnight trip ($150) goes to South Monomoy Island, where you'll sleep in the nineteenth-century lighthouse and keeper's cottage. For a current brochure and prices, write Cape Cod Museum of Natural History, Drawer R, Route 6A, Brewster 02631.

Orleans is another town that's chockablock with stores and restaurants. Two of the nicest stores, although they're no secrets, are right on Route 6A. The Birdwatcher's General Store (508–255–6974) is a bird-watcher's dream come true. Never in one store will you see so many birding items, from field guides and binoculars to feeders and fountains, prints and note cards, paintings and posters. Tree's Place (508–255–1330) is an art gallery and craft showroom in one. Fine regional paintings are on exhibit, while the shop has some lovely and high-quality goods, including pottery, jewelry, decorator ceramic tiles, art glass, and Russian lacquerware boxes.

Although there are plenty of upscale restaurants in Orleans, fishermen can feel right at home at Captain Cass Rock Harbor Seafood, on Rock Harbor Road (no phone), which is open June through October. Strung with buoys and nets, the restaurant looks like an old fishing shack, and you should be able to spill anything on its tables covered with black-and-white-checkered oilcloth or on its battered wooden floor. Lobster rolls ("no filler") are its specialty, along with fish, clam, and scallop plates.

One of the most spectacular ocean beaches for pounding surf and miles of dunes is Nauset Beach. You can walk there if you stay at the Nauset House Inn (508–255–2195), a bed-and-breakfast on Beach Road in East Orleans. This former nineteenth-century sea captain's home has plenty of spreading-out room for guests. Many reading nooks can be found in the airy, turn-of-the-century glass conservatory, filled with comfortable wicker and plants. The fourteen guest rooms are beautifully stenciled by the innkeeper, who is also an artist. Her hand-painted nightstands, mirrors, and chairs in Swiss motifs also decorate the rooms. Write to Nauset House Inn, P.O. Box 774, East Orleans 02643 (doubles, $55–$95).

Before you leave Orleans, step into the French Cable Station Museum at the corner of Cove Road and Route 28, built in 1890 to house the extension of the transatlantic cable from France to Eastham. A jumble of original equipment lies piled on tables in several rooms, and there are also historic photos of the cable being laid. The curators demonstrate how a cable message was translated from wavy lines to letters. News of the wreck of the paddle steamer *Portland* out of Boston arrived here first, as did news of Lindbergh's landing in Paris. The museum is open in July and August from 2:00 to 4:00 P.M. daily except Sunday. Tickets cost $1.00 for adults and 50 cents for children. Call (508) 240–1735.

Thousands of people visit the **Salt Pond Visitors Center of Cape Cod National Seashore** (508–255–3421), and you'll see why when you come. Wall-high windows offer striking vistas of Salt Pond and the surrounding coastline. The museum here is beautifully conceived and presented. There are excellent color photos of many native animals and birds, plus exhibits on such local industries as fishing, cranberrying, and whaling. The bookstore has a wide selection of field guides and natural history books, and the slide shows about Cape history and geography are well worth watching. Several nature trails lead off from the visitor center.

Despite the many visitors, most don't bother to sign up for the great variety of interpretive programs here, held daily in summer. You might follow in the footsteps of Henry David Thoreau, visit some retired lighthouses, or see a shellfishing demonstration. Another tour takes you to the Captain Edward Penniman House, an unusually ornate house built in 1867 for a New Bedford whaling captain and of French Second Empire style, with a mansard roof and an octagonal cupola. An arch made of whalebone jaws frames its entrance.

Wellfleet is called "the Art Gallery Town" because there are so many **art galleries** here, almost two dozen. They're clus-

Bayside Lobster Hutt

tered on Main Street or within a few blocks, and so you can
make a nice walking tour of them. Artists in every medium
are represented, and you'll see the work of nationally known
Cape artists as well as foreign artists. A popular tradition on
many Saturday nights is cocktail party openings, at which
you can meet the artists. Strolling about to these openings
on a warm summer night is a wonderful way to spend the
evening. For a guide to the galleries, write Wellfleet Art Galleries Association, P.O. Box 916, South Wellfleet 02667.

Many people like to top off their gallery tours with dinner
at one of the number of excellent and sophisticated (also
expensive) restaurants in town. A restaurant that is neither
expensive nor sophisticated is the Bayside Lobster Hutt
(508–349–6333), at the foot of Commercial Street, a former
oyster shack on the waterfront. You'll know you're there
when you see a man in a dory on the roof, hauling up a giant
lobster in a net. Service here is cafeteria-style, the floor is
concrete, and you sit at communal picnic tables. But you can
get some of the best and freshest lobster-in-the-rough you'll
ever eat, plus fish-and-chips, fried clams, shrimp, swordfish,
and bluefish.

Right across the parking lot from Bayside Lobster Hutt is a romantic, dessert-only alfresco restaurant called **Just Dessert.** Its white lattice and blue-and-white awnings look out on a sweeping view of sea grass and lagoon and weathered old shipwrecks. With the breeze blowing on a summer evening, dessert here is an experience. Choices range from simple to fancy: ice cream and sundaes, freshly baked hazelnut torte, and tropical lemon cake. The restaurant also serves coffee and pastries in the morning.

The Wellfleet Bay Wildlife Sanctuary (508-349-2615) is one of Massachusetts Audubon's largest and most active. Its 700 acres of pristine salt marsh, woods, fields, and brooks are fine places to wander, on 5 miles of nature trails. The program offerings are rich and of wide appeal. Besides birding and botany walks, there are canoe trips, sunset and whale-watching cruises, and family hikes. A three-hour cruise to Nauset Marsh takes you to the setting of *The Outermost House,* Henry Beston's book about a year spent living alone among the dunes. Nauset Marsh is also home to thousands of shorebirds and Massachusetts's largest tern colony. Hearty souls will love the **wintertime cruises** from January to April to see harbor and gray seals. Thousands of these playful-looking mammals winter off the Massachusetts coast. The fee is $30; reservations are required. Wellfleet Bay is on West Road, just off Route 6.

"Off the beaten path in Provincetown" is an oxymoron. Summer crowds jam this resort town so densely that people walk twelve abreast on Commercial Street. Still, P'town is a carnival of variety and audacity, its alternative lifestyles and dozens of galleries, boutiques, sophisticated restaurants, nightclubs, and arts offerings serving as a magnet for the masses. There's no other place like it in all of Massachusetts.

If the energy required on Commercial Street wears you down, drive out to **Race Point,** which never disappoints. The narrow road out to the lighthouse winds through dunes, and grasses and through hillsides covered with wind-beaten scrub. You can smell the salt heavy in the air and feel the cleansing wind in your face. In any season, no matter what the weather, Race Point is starkly wild and beautiful. Thoreau, who made a walking tour of the Cape in 1849, wrote that "a man may stand there and put all America behind him." So you may.

Another thing that never disappoints is **whale watching.**
Seeing these gentle giants up close is a moving experience,
one you'll never forget. Cruises go to Stellwagen Bank, the
whales' feeding grounds. There are a number of cruise lines
on the wharves, but the Dolphin Fleet boats are staffed by
scientists from the Center for Coastal Studies, experts in
whale research. The scientists have identified and named
several hundred humpback whales. Scientist-led cruises are
sensitive to the whales' behavior and are less likely to disturb
the creatures' feeding or breeding activities. The Dolphin
Fleet offers three cruises a day, from April through October,
leaving from Macmillan Wharf. Advance reservations are
advised in summer, especially on weekends. Fares are $15 to
$16 per person. Call (800) 826–9300 or (508) 255–3857.

P'town is a restaurant mecca, and some of the Cape's finest
eateries are here. There is such a wide choice that it's impossible to single out the most remarkable ones. Here are three
personal favorites: (1). Ciro & Sal's, at 4 Kiley Court, off 430
Commercial Street (508–487–0049), is a wonderful bastion to
the early days of P'town's unknown beginnings as an artists'
colony. Founded by two artists in the early 1950s, Ciro &
Sal's was opened in a dirt-floor basement down an alley, with
nail kegs for seats, a stove found at the town dump, and fishermen and artists as its first customers. Today you're more
likely to find tourists in the majority, but the rough wooden
beams hung with straw-covered Chianti bottles remain the
same, as does the excellent Italian cuisine. (2). A terrific
breakfast spot is the Cafe Edwige, at 333 Commercial Street
(508–487–2008). It's an airy, upstairs loft space with light
woods and paintings by local artists. Creative pancakes and
omelets are specialties, as are pastries and fruit and yogurt
dishes. There are also many take-out and snack places. (3). At
Juventino's Portuguese Bakery, at 338 Commercial Street
(508–487–1414), you can get Portuguese sweetbread, ele-
phant ears, or cinnamon walnut sticks to munch as you walk.

Martha's Vineyard

Closer to the mainland than Nantucket, Martha's Vineyard is
only forty-five minutes by ferry from Woods Hole. (For infor-

mation, call the Woods Hole, Martha's Vineyard, and Nantucket Steamship Authority [508–771–4000], which also services Nantucket. Summer car reservations must be made months in advance.) For complete travel information, contact the Martha's Vineyard Chamber of Commerce, Beach Road, P.O. Box 1698, Vineyard Haven 02568; (508) 693–0085.

The mass of tourists descend on Vineyard Haven, where the ferry docks. They also converge on Oak Bluffs, to see the Flying Horses Carousel, the nation's oldest, and the nineteenth-century gingerbread cottages and the Methodist Tabernacle. The rest of the island is generally less crowded. Shuttle buses service the island in summer. If you have a sturdy pair of legs, you can bike about—the island is 20 miles long and 10 miles wide.

A short distance from the ferry terminal is an island institution, the Black Dog Tavern, at Beach Street Extension (508–693–9223), with a seaside porch dining room. Local seafood dishes, meats, and freshly baked breads and desserts from its own bakery are offered.

More spacious and sprightly than your average pizza house, Papa's Pizza on Circuit Avenue in Oak Bluffs (508–693–1400) has plenty of tables, bright red walls and a tin ceiling, and antique posters and prints. The self-service menu lets you choose from a long list of toppings.

Just outside of Oak Bluffs is a bed-and-breakfast at a far enough remove to be quiet at night, the Admiral Benbow Inn (508–693–6825 or 800–331–1787). A gray-shingled, Queen Anne Victorian that rises to a stately cupola, the inn exudes the warmth of hospitable innkeepers and antique oak furnishings. Gorgeous original oak moldings, hefty doors, and bay windows complement the seven rooms with private baths. More period touches, such as floral wallpapers, pedestal sinks, and oak armoires, lend old-fashioned charm. The parlor and dining room and the sunny porch with white wicker chairs are comfortable spaces, and breakfast is a feast that covers two mahogany sideboards. Some of the highlights are freshly baked lemon bread, croissants, and French toast with bacon. Write the inn at P.O. Box 2488, Oak Bluffs 02557 (double, $40–$90).

As you tour Martha's Vineyard, it may surprise you to see a white-tailed deer or a wild turkey cross the road. But the island is a great haven for wildlife, and one of its most stunning achievements is the osprey nesting program. You can see the 40-foot poles erected as nesting platforms for these huge birds at Felix Neck Wildlife Sanctuary on the Edgartown–Vineyard Haven Road (508–627–4850). From two breeding pairs in 1971, their numbers had by 1990 grown to almost eighty pairs; in 1989 the osprey was removed from the list of endangered species, the first in Massachusetts removed because of recovery. There's also a small museum as well as nature trails.

Another place to enjoy the out-of-doors that's a more remote preserve is **Cedar Tree Neck.** A car-disabling dirt road leads to a tiny parking lot; a short wooded trail, to the beach. An almost-constant wind has twisted the trees into intriguingly blasted-looking shapes. Finally you come upon a peaceful vista of sand and dunes and bayberry, circling a lagoon, especially nice at sunset. Take Indian Hill Road off State Road several miles west of Vineyard Haven.

Quintessential Martha's Vineyard is expressed by the Field Gallery, an art gallery in a field in the center of West Tisbury. Some twenty larger-than-life, dancing white figures inhabit the lawn. They look slightly Picassoesque, with their thick rounded limbs and curving forms. There are a massive chicken with a tiny head, a figure blowing a trumpet, a hatted figure with a little dog, and a colonial figure on horseback. The sculptures are the work of island artist Tom Maley, who exhibits the work of others in the adjacent gallery. The Field Gallery is such an island institution that people like to get married here.

A surprising amount of Martha's Vineyard is farmland. Goats, sheep, cows, vegetables, and fruits are husbanded by entrepreneurs who like island living as much as their independence. Llamas are raised at **Takemmy Farm** (508–693–2486), one of only a handful of llama farms in New England, on State Road in Vineyard Haven. The farm also produces and sells honey, maple syrup, mulch, hay, and yarn and offers animal visits from 1:00 to 5:00 P.M. Wednesday and Saturday.

The Allen Farm on South Road in Chilmark has been a family farm since the seventeenth century, and Allens still run it, these days keeping a herd of some seventy New Zealand sheep. The wool goes into gorgeous hand-knit sweaters of a comforting weight, as well as scarves, hats, and shawls—all sold in a sunny gift shop behind a neat stone wall. Call (508) 645–9064.

Pick-your-own raspberries is the big attraction at Thimble. Farm (508–693–6396), on the Edgartown–Vineyard Haven Road in Vineyard Haven. Ever-bearing varieties extend picking throughout the summer and most of the fall.

The road to **Menemsha** winds through field and forest and ends abruptly at a stone wall that could pitch you right into the sea. In this miniature fishing village with a tiny harbor are more boats than houses. The village has a post office, a fish market, a restaurant, and a gas station, and that's about it. A small beach facing due west is a popular spot for celebrating the sunset, one of few places on the East Coast where the sun sinks into the sea. (Key West, stand aside.)

While busloads of tourists tramp the path to the **Gay Head Cliffs,** these spectacular white chalk cliffs should not be missed. They run for 1 mile along the coast, with a dramatic backdrop of russet-colored beach vegetation and the stout, handsome brick spire of the Gay Head Light. The cliffs were the country's first registered Natural Landmark.

Nantucket

Nantucket is somehow even more an island than Martha's Vineyard. Isolated 20 or so miles at sea, it's two and a half hours by ferry from the mainland. If you get stranded by a winter gale (and people do), you're really stranded. Because of its flat terrain and smaller size—14 miles long by 3½ miles wide—the island is manageable on a bike, which gets you outside the crowded town of Nantucket. There are also buses and taxis. For complete travel information, contact the Nantucket Island Chamber of Commerce, Pacific Club Building, Nantucket 02554; (508) 228–1700.

Maria Mitchell was the nation's first woman astronomer. The king of Denmark awarded Maria a gold medal in 1847 when she discovered a comet. She was born in a typical Quaker house built in 1790, a two-story dwelling with weathered shingles on Vestal Street. Now it's the **Maria Mitchell Science Center and Birthplace.** The small rooms of the family home have plain plaster walls and some Mitchell family memorabilia. Adjacent to the birthplace are a science library and natural science museum containing native flora and fauna and offering nature walks; in summer, Wednesday nights are "star nights" at the nearby Loines Observatory. The birthplace and museum are open from 10:00 A.M. to 4:00 P.M. Tuesday through Saturday, mid-June through August. Admission is $3.00 for adults and $1.50 for children (separate fees are charged for the birthplace and the museum). Call (508) 228–9198.

An often-overlooked spot a short distance from town is the **Nantucket Lifesaving Museum,** a replica of the 1874 lifesaving station. Years ago, shoal-bound Nantucket harvested so many wrecks that it was called "the Graveyard of the Atlantic." A newspaper clipping recounts the dramatic, 1829 rescue of the crew of the *H. P. Kirkham,* 15 miles offshore in a winter storm. Sepia-toned old photos show other wrecks and a horse-drawn lifeboat on the beach. Quarterboards hang on the walls—ships' wooden nameplates with gold letters and elaborately carved floral designs. The museum is 2½ miles out on the Polpis Road, on the left by a marsh. It's easy to miss by car, but on a bike you'll quickly spot the white stone marker with the museum's name at the entrance. Hours are 9:30 A.M. to 4:30 P.M. daily, June 15 to September 15. Entrance costs $1.50.

Despite this island's tiny size, fully one-third of it has been set aside as open space by the Nantucket Conservation Foundation and the Nantucket Land Bank. Their actions ensure that the island's fragile beauty will be protected from the heavy pressures of tourism and development. One such property is Sanford Farm, a great place for hiking, out on Madaket Road. Out the Polpis Road, just past the Wauwinet Road turnoff, is the Windswept Cranberry Bog, a small working bog where you can watch the harvest in season. Hearty hikers will love **Eel Point,** a wild, wind-ripped barrier sand spit at the northwest tip of the island. Trails lead through dunes, salt marshes, and tidal flats, where there is a wide variety of wildlife and birds. Four-wheel drives are allowed here too, but not many come. The currents are too dangerous for swimming. A guide and map to Eel Point are available from the Maria Mitchell Association (see pg. 80). For a map of land bank properties, write the Nantucket Land Bank Commission, 18 Broad Street, Nantucket 02554, or call (508) 228–7240. The Nantucket Conservation Foundation, at 118 Cliff Road, Nantucket 02554 (508–228–2884), sells a guide to its properties for about $3.00.

A scattering of quaint, interesting villages dots the island. Siasconset, called **Sconset** for short, began as a fishing village of one-room shacks in the seventeenth century. Sconset's tiny, weathered cottages cluster together like a dollhouse village, festooned with rambling roses—a pretty sight in summer. There's a nice public beach but few conveniences besides a gas station, market, and post office. Nonetheless, the island's best restaurant, Chanticleer (508–257–6231), is here, serving classic French cuisine in a rose-covered cottage (closed in winter). Another small village is Quidnet, reached from the Polpis Road; take the first unmarked left past Wauwinet Road. A one-lane road quickly turns to rutted sand, coming upon a few small, weathered cottages overlooking a large pond and the ocean. A strip of beach between the pond and the ocean is Conservation Foundation property and offers a view of Sankaty Light (no parking).

A change of pace from the expensive downtown boutiques of the town of Nantucket is Bartlett's Ocean View Farm (508–228–9403), off Hummock Pond Road on Bartlett Farm Road. Its greenhouses offer a wide array of excellent produce, including ten kinds of lettuce. The island's mild falls mean you can buy tomatoes in November, and December finds the staff still picking broccoli.

There are dozens of restaurants on Nantucket and, in general, better restaurants than on Martha's Vineyard. In Nantucket town, there's a restaurant on every block, and the only hard part is choosing one. Here are two you might try: The Brotherhood of Thieves, at 23 Broad Street (no phone; no reservations), has a tavernlike atmosphere, with dark woods, romantic lighting, and the warmth of a fireplace. People willingly stand in line for its burgers, sandwiches almost too thick to eat, and curly shoestring fries, served on pewter plates. At dinner there are grilled fish dishes and steaks as well. On the outskirts of town, the Beach Plum Cafe and Bakery, at 11 West Creek Road (508–228–8893), has a summery feel, with its light woods and white walls hung with Nantucket watercolors. Breakfasts offer freshly baked breads, croissants, and pastries from the restaurant bakery next door; omelets; and pancakes. Lunches include deli sandwiches, warm and cold salads, and black bean chili. A variety of meat and fish dishes rounds out the dinner menu.

For a quick coffee and snack in town, stop into the Espresso Cafe, at 40 Main Street (508–228–6930), where a self-service counter dispenses great home-baked cookies, breads, and desserts to go, with espresso and cappuccino. There's also a good selection of homemade soups and unusual sandwiches, such as grilled gouda with apple chutney on egg-dipped bread. In season, you can sit out on the garden patio.

Someone once suggested to innkeeper Mary Kay Condon that a tavern called the Stagger Out be built next door to her bed-and-breakfast, the Stumble Inne. So far, no one has done so, but the inn still has the most unpretentious name in town. A short distance from the hustle and bustle of town, it's quiet at night. The Greek Revival house was built in 1704 by a whaling family. Its high ceilings, tall windows, and oak moldings have been complemented by jewel-like paint colors and exquisitely chosen antiques. In the dining room is a 6-foot, marble-topped oak sideboard with a mirrored shelf and heavy relief carvings of owls' heads and griffins. The sideboard holds the buffet breakfast: yogurt, granola, home-baked apple or cranberry muffins, fruits, and juices. Guest rooms have lace curtains, four-posters, or white iron bedsteads, as well as handmade quilts, and are furnished with antiques. There are six more rooms across the street in an early nineteenth-century Quaker half-house. Write to the inn at 109 Orange Street, Nantucket 02554, or call (508) 228–4482 (doubles, $35–$115, depending on the season and whether you share a bath).

Off the Beaten Path in Southeastern Massachusetts

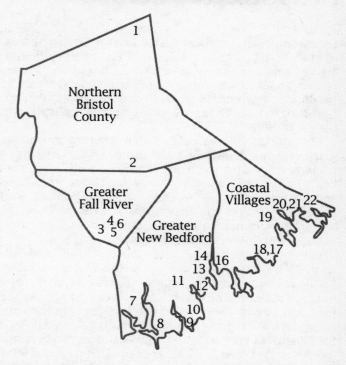

Northern Bristol County

Greater Fall River

Coastal Villages

Greater New Bedford

1. Buildings designed by
   Henry Hobson Richardson
2. Dighton Rock State Park
3. Fall River Heritage
   State Park
4. Factory outlets
5. Columbia Street
6. Ukrainian Home restaurant
7. Scenic drive
8. The Bayside
9. Lloyd Center for
   Environmental Studies
10. Salvador's Icecream
11. Children's Museum
12. Padanaram

13. Fishermen's Wharf
14. Rotch-Jones-Duff
    House & Garden Museum
15. Cuttyhunk Island
16. Walking tour of
    Poverty Point
17. Mattapoisett waterfront
18. Mattapoisett Historical
    Society Museum and
    Carriage House
19. Jonathan's Sprouts
20. Fearing Tavern
21. Tremont Nail Company
22. Victorian waterfront in
    Onset Bay

Southeastern Massachusetts

Southeastern Massachusetts, or Bristol County, holds some of the prettiest and most unspoiled territory in the state. Tucked into a corner between Rhode Island and Plymouth, it encompasses miles and miles of farmland, where quiet cornfields line both sides of the road. Small rural towns like Dighton, Rehoboth, and Berkley appear as little surprises here and there.

The coastal villages east of New Bedford are picturesque gems. Founded mostly by shipbuilders, they're proud of their history and have preserved it well. These villages became favored summer resorts for residents of New York and Boston, among them Oliver Wendell Holmes, who summered in Mattapoisett. In Marion, you can still see the great Victorian summer homes erected along a long waterfront avenue, with broad acres of lawns.

The most high-profile cities are Fall River and New Bedford. Both have prestigious pasts. Fall River led the world in textile production in the nineteenth century, and many of its old mill buildings now serve as offices and shops. New Bedford was one of the greatest whaling ports in the world and today has a lingering flavor of whaling's heyday in its historic district's cobblestoned streets and gas-style lamps. Both Fall River and New Bedford are famous for their factory outlets, Fall River's more of the everyday variety, New Bedford's of the Calvin Klein stripe.

For complete travel information, contact the Bristol County Development Council, 70 North Second Street, P.O. Box BR-976, New Bedford 02741; (508) 997–1250.

Northern Bristol County

As you walk or drive about North Easton, it's a little startling to see Gothic behemoths of stone, complete with gargoyles, looming from every corner. Altogether, there are five **build-**

ings designed by Henry Hobson Richardson, as well as nine landscapings by Frederick Law Olmsted, three Augustus Saint-Gaudens sculptures, two John La Farge stained-glass windows, and three National Historic districts—such wealth that architects come from Chicago and Australia just to see it.

How did it happen? It all goes back to Oliver Ames, who founded the world's largest shovel company here in the early 1800s. By 1850, more than 60 percent of all the world's shovels were Ames shovels. During the Civil War, President Lincoln personally asked Oliver Ames to supply the Union Army with his shovels. Ames's descendants subsequently shoveled the profits into elaborate mansions and civic gifts, commissioning Richardson. One such building is the Old Colony Railroad Station on Mechanic Street, which serves as a town history museum. Here you can get a walking/driving-tour map. The towering Oakes Ames Memorial Hall and the Oliver Ames Free Library on Center Street are also HHR creations. Besides these larger structures, Richardson designed a stone Gate Lodge and a shingled Gardener's Cottage. The museum is open from 2:00 to 4:00 P.M. the second Sunday of every month. For information, write the Easton Historical Society, Box 3, North Easton 02356, or call the curator at (508) 238–3143.

Across the banks of the Taunton River to the east is a large rock with ancient inscriptions on it, a rock whose origins have mystified scientists for three centuries. It's displayed under glass in a small white pavilion in **Dighton Rock State Park** in Berkley. The faded characters are definitely there, kind of pointy- and hieroglyphic-looking. But who wrote them? More than twenty theories have been advanced. The front-runners, explained in large panels, are that the marks originated from American Indians, Phoenicians, Vikings, or Portuguese explorers. The park overlooks the Taunton River, with picnic tables in the shade. Call (508) 644–5522 for hours and information. To get to the park, take exit 10 from Route 24 and follow the signs.

Greater Fall River

Antique beds are nice things to buy, except for the fact that they don't come in queen or double. But at Leonard's

Antiques, you can get an antique bed resized to a custom fit. Leonard's stocks hundreds of antique beds, from late 1700s–era beds to Victorian ones, ranging in price from about $1,000 to as much as $12,000. The shop is at 600 Taunton Avenue in Seekonk; call (508) 336–8585.

Busloads of Liberace fans seek out the Polish Princess Keyboard Museum in Swansea. The "museum" is actually more of an unabashed, Las Vegas–style temple to the concert career of Carolyn Lee, a.k.a. "the Polish Princess," than it is a tribute to Liberace. But she was friends with Liberace, and she has some Liberace memorabilia, crammed into the back of her music shop in a strip mall with a three-ton concrete piano outside. Brightly lighted mirrors, chandeliers, and candelabra-bedecked pianos showcase the pictures and such that she collected. The Polish Princess is a female version of Liberace, with her long blond mane and cloud of rhinestones, lamé, and sequins. The museum is located at 1211 G.A.R. Highway (Route 6); call (508) 678–2900 for hours. Before paying admission, though, think hard about how much you really love Liberace: tickets cost $3.50 for adults and $2.50 for students.

Fall River lost its lead as a textile producer to low-cost southern labor. The story of the city's great rise and fall in prosperity is told at the **Fall River Heritage State Park,** designed to look like an old mill in an eight-acre waterfront setting. From a farm village, the city grew rapidly to more than a hundred mills, and production easily outstripped that of competitors Lawrence and Lowell. Poignant black-and-white photographs show the immigrant mill workers, many of whom were children. A slide show tells the moving history of the many ethnic groups who powered the mills. The park is at 200 Davol Street West, next to Battleship Cove. Call (508) 675–5759 for current hours.

Fall River claims it has the largest center of **factory outlets** in New England: eighty outlets in three large buildings on Quequechan and Quarry streets, complete with cafeterias and delis so that you can shop all day. Besides the usual children's, women's, and men's clothing, the shops also sell handbags, jewelry, candy, party goods, crafts, fabric, cosmetics, linens, and books. Brand names include Farberware, Corning/Revere, Carter's, London Fog, Bali, Izod, and Converse. To get there, take exit 8A from I–195 to Route 24 south. Get off at exit 2, Brayton Avenue, and follow the signs marked with a heart. Call the "shopper's hotline" at (508) 678–6033 for information. You can also write for a free guide from the Fall River Factory Outlet District Association, P.O. Box 2877, Fall River 02722.

Among the many ethnic groups of mill workers were large waves of Portuguese and Polish, who left a lasting imprint on the city. The Portuguese have a home-front stronghold on **Columbia Street,** complete with eight-sided cobblestones and black iron lampposts. Old ladies in black with lace mantillas walk along with bowed heads; laundry hangs between the triple-decker houses, and the street is redolent with Portuguese bakeries, fish markets, coffee shops, and restaurants. The heart of Columbia Street is Chaves Market (508–672–7821), where almost every customer speaks in the lilting tones of Portuguese. You can buy almost anything Portuguese here: octopus, conch shells, *chourico,* sugar-coated almonds, *vinho verde,* Portuguese cookies and sweetbread, paella pans, and porcelain samovars and centerpieces.

You could not find a more low-key place to get good Polish food than the **Ukrainian Home** restaurant (popularly called "the Uke"). Situated downstairs in a beat-up old yellow brick building that saw better days before you were born, it has a grottolike darkness punctuated only by red and green ship's running lights and neon fish. It's been a fishermen's haunt since the 1950s, and their stuffed fish hang on the walls. Polish and Ukrainian delicacies include cabbage soup, *golumbki,* pirogi, kielbasa, and stuffed cabbage rolls, along with *chourico* sandwiches, all at moderate prices. The Uke is at 482 Globe Street; call (508) 672–9677.

For a truly **scenic drive,** exit Route 6 at Route 88 and follow it south to Kirby Road, to begin a driving tour that makes a natural loop around the Westport River, bringing you to Dartmouth. Along the way, you'll see farms with silver silos, stone walls, pastureland sloping to the sea, and several great finds in country restaurants (pick one for lunch). Turn right on Kirby Road, and then turn left onto Main Road, which brings you through the center of Westport, past its town hall and Quaker Meeting House. Shortly afterward, you'll come to Fred & Ann's Restaurant, at 977 Main Road (508–636–4622), a real country eatery with knotty-pine paneling, paper place mats, and institution-weight white crockery. Plain old goodies like baked ham, fish-and-chips, and beef liver with bacon pack people in daily. Bountiful portions mean you must budget for dessert, perhaps one of seventeen kinds of pie. (The restaurant is closed Mondays and Tuesdays.)

Main Road becomes Westport Point Road as it approaches Westport Point Village, as quaint as its seafaring origins. On a little warren of tiny streets rise eighteenth- and nineteenth-century sea captains' houses, all dated and identified with signs.

Go back up to Drift Road on the right, and take it over to Route 88 south. Just after the bridge over the inlet, the first right brings you to a little joint called Jerome's Moby Dick Sandwich Shop. In this brick bunker with blue picnic tables outside and a little counter and some tables inside, you can get great lobster, baked fish, and spaghetti, among other things. Route 88 ends just before Horseneck Beach, a spectacular beach fronting the ocean on a narrow peninsula at the mouth of the Westport River. Leave the peninsula via East Beach Road, which brings you east of the river to Horseneck Road. Up on the left, with a panoramic view of sweeping pastureland that stretches unbroken down to the sea, is **The Bayside,** at 1253 Horseneck Road (508–636–5882), another great country restaurant. This one bills itself as "the best dinky little restaurant in the Commonwealth." And dinky it is—you can traverse its narrow dining room in two steps. Wide windows let you admire the view. Everything is "made from scratch," from sandwiches and burgers with handcut french fries to pan-fried smelt and homemade pies.

Greater New Bedford

From Horseneck Road, turn right onto Slade Corner Road, which brings you into the historic little village of Russells Mills, a neighborhood of South Dartmouth. The village is home to Salt Marsh Pottery, now sold all over the country. This pottery features pretty designs made with real wildflowers imprinted in clay and painted. The studio and showroom are downstairs in a 1913 schoolhouse, where you can buy the bowls, plates, tiles, and lamps made in this style. The showroom is at 1167 Russells Mills Road; call (508) 636–4813.

If you backtrack from Russells Mills Road and go left onto Rock 'O Dundee Road, it will bring you to Potomska Road and the **Lloyd Center for Environmental Studies.** This is really a hidden jewel. Set on the picturesque Slocums River Estuary, its coastal zone habitat makes it an amateur naturalist's and birder's paradise. You can wander the salt marshes, swamps, and forests on a handful of nature trails. On the research building's third floor, an observation deck gives lordly views of the estuarine lowlands, Buzzards Bay, and the Elizabeth Islands. Inside are low-key and casual exhibits on native wildlife and water pollution, along with the skeleton of a pilot whale. Beautiful photographs show the river and species of birds and butterflies. Downstairs is a roomful of aquariums and a tide-pool tank. A wide variety of educational and natural history–oriented programs is offered. The center is at 430 Potomska Road; call (508) 990–0505. Hours are 9:00 A.M. to 5:00 P.M. daily except Monday (the grounds are open daily).

Continuing out on the neck of land that is Dartmouth, follow Little River Road to Smith Neck Road and turn left for three more interesting stops. On your right, at the sign for Round Hill Condominiums, look down toward the ocean. You'll see a rambling stone mansion that was built by the son of Hetty Green, the fabled "Witch of Wall Street." Heiress to a New Bedford whaling and shipping family fortune, she shrewdly invested her way to one of the largest personal fortunes in the country by the turn of the century. Hetty was a miserly sort, dressing in tattered black rags. She was so miserly, in fact, that when her son broke his leg she refused him a doctor, and he became crippled for life. Perhaps partly for revenge, the son and his sister spent their mother's money into the ground. Building the mansion, which rivals those of Newport, certainly helped. Now it's condominiums. You can also see it from Round Hill Beach in the off-season (October to May), when you can drive down the condominium access road to the beach.

Just up the road a piece on the left, you'll come to a giant brown wooden milk bottle with yellow-and-white awnings. It's **Salvador's Icecream,** a vintage lunch stand built in 1936. Now it dispenses cones, dishes, sundaes, burgers, *linguica,* and grinders, at the edge of a pasture with grazing sheep. The stand is at 460 Smith Neck Road; call (508) 994–4193. It's open daily Easter to Columbus Day.

Smith Neck was named after Captain John Smith, who explored the neck and owned land here in 1665. Some of that land belongs to a Smith descendant, Sally Brownell, who has opened her home as a bed-and-breakfast inn called Salt Marsh Farm. It was a working farm in the 1800s, and today the 200-year-old Federal farmhouse wears a patina of being well used. The wide-planked floorboards creak a bit, and you may have to stoop to get through the low, narrow doorways. Old etchings and paintings adorn the walls, and handmade yellow quilts grace the rooms. A special aspect of this inn is the nature trail that winds through its ninety acres of hay fields, forest, salt meadows, and tidal marshes. Write Brownell at 322 Smith Neck Road, South Dartmouth 02748, or call (508) 992–0980 (two rooms, each with private bath; $60–$75 double).

Smith Neck Road ends at Gulf Road. If you take a right, you'll wind up in the village of Padanaram. But a short detour left will bring you to the **Children's Museum,** an unusual resource in a town this small. It's housed in an antique barn, with weathered silos still attached. "Please touch" is the message here, on two floors of hands-on exhibits. Everything is bright, cheerful, and colorful, from the balloons on the ceiling to the aquarium built into a fuchsia-and-green arcade. Play areas galore fill both floors: among them a crawling tube, a model car, and cutouts of fairy-tale characters that kids can put their faces in. Outside you can enjoy nature trails and picnic tables. The museum is at 276 Gulf Road; call (508) 993-3361 for information. Hours are from 10:00 A.M. to 5:00 P.M. Tuesday through Saturday and from 1:00 to 5:00 P.M. Sunday. Admission is $3.75.

The village of **Padanaram** is so sprightly and chic that you'll ask what it's doing in an old Yankee boat-building town. Padanaram is home to the world-famous wooden yacht company Concordia, and yachtspeople from all over the globe put in to port. Along two tiny blocks of Elm Street cluster some fine shops and restaurants that make for a nice stroll. Among the wares are Icelandic sweaters, dollhouses, antiques, handcrafted furniture, and china and gifts.

If you've planned your time right, stop at 302 Elm Street to have lunch at Capers, a gourmet bakery and deli that also puts up take-out and picnic fixings (508–996–2440). The food is so good here that you're tempted to load up with a lot of it. Well, who can turn down a slice of chocolate fudge rum butter cake, anyway? Hearty sandwiches made on French bread are filled with smoked turkey, smoked salmon, and goat cheese, among other offerings, and feature such trimmings as mango chutney, Greek olives, sun-dried tomatoes, and honey-cup mustard. Beautifully made cakes and cookies line the bakery counter.

At dinnertime, a favored haunt is the Bridge Street Cafe, at 10A Bridge Street (508–994–7200)—a casual bistro that is faintly Casablancaesque with its papier-mâché tropical birds hanging from the ceiling. The menu changes every two days, but it always features knockout dishes of grilled and barbecued seafoods and meats, nightly prix fixe specials, and some Mexican dishes. Lunch offers homemade soups, salads, and sandwiches.

New Bedford's whaling heritage is much in evidence at the Whaling Museum and along the restored waterfront. But the city is still a working port today, with the nation's most productive fishing fleet. For a taste of salt air and a view of these colorfully painted ships berthed at their moorings, walk out on **Fishermen's Wharf.** Starting early in the afternoon, the boats return to port, shadowed by clouds of screaming gulls.

Many fishermen are Portuguese, just as they were in the nineteenth century, and the city's North End is thickly lined with Portuguese bakeries and bridal shops. Here you'll find Cafe Mimo, an intimate Portuguese restaurant where the Old World is still very much alive. Amid the stucco walls and hanging plants of the cafe, the sound of Portuguese is a natural one. The menu lists lots of traditional offerings, such as shrimp Mocambique, barbecued sardines, and grilled quail, all at moderate prices. Cafe Mimo serves breakfast, lunch, and dinner daily and is at 1528 Acushnet Avenue; call (508) 996–9443.

If you're in the waterfront district and hungry, look for Phoebe's Restaurant (508–999–5486), a warm and cozy neighborhood restaurant with pink cafe curtains and black lunch-counter stools. It's at 288 Union Street, just a few blocks from the Whaling Museum. The good homemade food and low prices pack people in for breakfast and lunch. If you've never had French toast made with Portuguese sweetbread, now's the time. A blackboard lists daily specials of omelets and pancakes, sandwiches and burgers. Homemade desserts include chocolate cake and two-tone pie.

Here's one more restaurant choice, for the seafood lover: Davy's Locker, at 1480 Rodney French Boulevard (508–992–7359), where the portions are large and the prices are right.

When Herman Melville described New Bedford's "brave houses and flowery gardens" in *Moby Dick,* he surely had the **Rotch-Jones-Duff House & Garden Museum** in mind. This house was designed in 1834 for William Rotch, Jr., a prominent whaling merchant, and was later owned by two other families. It stands out as one of the nation's finest examples of the Greek Revival style and is one of few left in the city that hasn't been converted to office space. The interior reflects the owners' histories via period antiques from the mid-nineteenth century into the twentieth. You wander from Victorian parlors with Italian marble fireplaces and gold-leaf mirrors to Mr. Rotch's opulent Greek Revival sitting room. Other house appointments include silk linens, eighteenth-century furniture, and a collection of Fabergé-style eggs made by Mrs. Duff. The grounds showcase a wildflower walk, a dogwood *allée,* and a boxwood parterre garden with pink, white, and red roses. In summer, concerts of acoustic music are held on the grounds. The house, located at 396 County Street, is open for tours from 11:00 A.M. to 4:00 P.M. Tuesday through Saturday, Memorial Day through September. Off-season hours are from 9:30 A.M. to 5:00 P.M. Tuesday through Friday or from 11:00 A.M. to 3:00 P.M. Saturdays by appointment. Admission is $3.00; call (508) 997–1401.

Much of downtown New Bedford is noisy and busy. But in a quiet section of largely Victorian houses, the Melville House B & B is a haven. Herman Melville's sister lived in this Italianate Victorian with its trios of arched windows. Melville visited her here and sat for his portrait. The innkeeper is a former protégé of Paul Prudhomme and loves cooking elaborate breakfasts. These might be a baked apple stuffed with oatmeal and cranberries or an oven pancake with Romano sauce and string beans. Breakfast is served in the solarium, a blaze of light with its many windows. Guest rooms are spacious and furnished with antiques, and each has a Carrara marble fireplace. The bath is shared. Write the inn at 100 Madison Street, New Bedford 02740; or call (508) 990–1566 (doubles, $65).

Though the Elizabeth Islands are mostly privately owned, there is one you can visit: **Cuttyhunk Island,** the westernmost of the chain that dangles off of Woods Hole. The ferry *M. V. Alert* leaves for Cuttyhunk from New Bedford's Pier 3 (508–992–1432) daily in summer, less often in spring and fall. A handful of people live on this tiny island. There is only one inn, and only one store. Once you land, you'll be surprised by the quiet, since few vehicles survive out here. Narrow village lanes wind uphill past weathered cottages and stone walls. A long paved path lined with stone walls like a European rampart leads to the summit, which offers a commanding view of the harbor, Buzzards Bay, and the nearby islands. Cuttyhunk is a lovely, unspoiled place, with small, secluded beaches and acres of windswept grasses and bayberry.

Right across the harbor from New Bedford is Fairhaven, an often-overlooked place. Fairhaven flourished in the eighteenth century as a shipbuilding town, supplying whaling ships to the burgeoning trade out of New Bedford. The original settlement area, called Poverty Point, constitutes several blocks centered on West, Cherry, and Oxford streets, situated off Main Street north of Route 6. Many weathered old houses of the ship chandlers, merchants, and shipwrights of that time still stand. One is a bed-and-breakfast, Edgewater Bed & Breakfast, originally built in the 1760s by a merchant who supplied the whaling and shipbuilding industries and later added onto, in the 1880s. Edgewater sits on a point of land overlooking the New Bedford Harbor scene. The water views from inside the house are splendidly set off by large, arched windows with inviting window seats. At night, the harbor lights make a pretty picture too. Rooms in the newer part of the house are larger and have nice antique touches, such as patterned wallpaper, a pencil four-poster, and a claw-foot bathtub. Rooms in the older section are smaller and more cramped, but nice too. Each has a private bath. Write the inn at 2 Oxford Street, Fairhaven 02719, or call (508) 997–5512 (doubles, $45–$65, with breakfast).

A **walking tour of Poverty Point** takes you to some of

the old whaling houses and turns up several interesting historical sites, such as where Joshua Slocum, the first man to circumnavigate the globe solo, set sail in 1895. (Edgewater innkeeper Betty Reed has brochures on the walking tour.) Elsewhere in Fairhaven, there are architectural treasures given to the town by millionaire Henry Huttleston Rogers. One is the Unitarian Memorial Church, one of the finest examples of English Gothic architecture in America.

Coastal Villages

Mattapoisett was once famous the world over for its whaling ships and built ships of all kinds for more than a century, with six shipyards lining the waterfront. Mattapoisett men made the ship *Acushnet,* on which Herman Melville crewed in 1840. The **Mattapoisett waterfront** is quiet now. But it's an attractive one, and a few wood-and-shingled eighteenth- and nineteenth-century houses still stand along narrow little Water Street. All have neatly lettered black-and-white signs identifying the owner and date: the 1798 carpenter's shop, the 1832 block shop. A small green park, Shipyard Park, looks out on the harbor. Right across the street is the Mattapoisett Inn (508–758–4922), a rambling old white seaside inn full of old-style resort ambience. Lace curtains and dark wood paneling decorate several of its dining rooms, and the front rooms have full harbor views. You can dine on the screened porch in summer. A less expensive cafe and bistro menu features salads, burgers, and sandwiches, as well as such specialties as chicken and apple croissants with melted cheddar. The American and Continental dinner menu lists grilled meats and seafood. Lots of live entertainment means the dining rooms can be noisy, but this is a much-loved place.

Town history is on view at the **Mattapoisett Historical Society Museum and Carriage House,** 1 block up at 5 Church Street (508–758–2844). The museum is housed in an 1821 church with pews and pulpits, an interesting backdrop. The collection, mostly donated by town residents, varies strikingly. Sea captains brought back such exotic things as Pacific seashells; silk and feather fans from many countries; a Chinese lacquered writing desk; and two painted and gilded glasses used by Napoleon on Saint Helena. Military memorabilia span the revolutionary war, the Civil War, and the War of 1812. Up on the balconies ranges a collection of dolls and toys, period furniture, and a stand full of antique canes, many with ivory tops. An attached building holds antique vehicles and farm tools, among them carriages and buggies, the town's first water wagon, a corn sheller, a bean winnower, a cranberry separator, and a corn chopper. The museum is open from 1:00 to 4:30 P.M. Tuesday through Saturday, July 5 to August 31. Admission is $2.00.

Never mind how many cornfields you pass in southeastern Massachusetts, there's a crop of a different color growing in Rochester—sprouts. At **Jonathan's Sprouts** on Vaughn's Hill Road (off Route 105, past the Rochester Golf Club) you can have a free tour and see the company's unique "flood and drain" system. In the plant with its concrete floors, everything is wet and dripping. Sprouts grow entirely in water, with no dirt. Mung beans are first soaked in bathtubs scattered about and then packed into giant metal tubes, where they are repeatedly doused with water. Here in the dark, the bean sprouts grow in only three days, doubling daily in volume like vegetables run amok in a science fiction horror flick. On Sundays, you can watch the harvesting and packaging from about 6:00 A.M. to about 3:00 P.M. Regular tours are given daily from 10:00 A.M. to 2:00 or 3:00 P.M. Call (800) 763–2577 or (508) 763–2577 for reservations.

Continuing east along the coast brings you to Wareham. The first stop here is the **Fearing Tavern,** believed to be Wareham's oldest house. This tavern played a large and long role in town history. The original lean-to part of the house dates to 1690. In 1765, Benjamin Fearing enlarged it and created a taproom, where town business was conducted and stagecoach travelers stopped; one small room was the town post office. The story has it that a British soldier hid in a secret closet in the tavern for three days. And during the War of 1812, more than 200 British marines marched to the tavern before burning a cotton factory. The house's third section was built after 1800. As you tour the house, you skip back and forth between centuries, from the taproom and parlor up to the second-story ell and bedrooms. Rooms are furnished with many period antiques and lots of original Fearing family possessions. The taproom still has its original painted green grille, a beautiful thing with an arched top and spindles carved in the shape of rope turnings. The tavern, located on Elm Street, is open from 1:00 to 4:00 P.M. July 4 weekend through Labor Day. Admission is $3.00 for adults and $1.00 for children.

Just down the street from the Fearing Tavern, at 8 Elm Street, is the **Tremont Nail Company,** the nation's oldest nail factory, listed on the National Register of Historic Places. Using hundred-year-old nail machines, the company still makes old-fashioned nails from cut sheets of high carbon steel, rolled and tempered. Cut nails can penetrate any wood without splitting it and have better holding power. The company was founded in 1819, and the current mill dates to 1848. Although there are no tours, you can look in the windows any weekday from 7:30 A.M. to 5:00 P.M. and hear the rumbling and chugging of the nail-cutting machines. The mill is still warmed by a few potbellied stoves. The full line of nails is sold across the street in the Company Store, formerly the cooper shop. Nails, running from a ¾-inch clout nail to an 8-inch boat spike, include rosehead, clinch, fine finish, and wrought-head. The store also sells colonial-style hardware, paints, gifts, and penny candy. A film explains the company history and a little bit about nailmaking. Outside the factory is a herring run. Call (508) 295–0038 for information.

Before leaving Wareham, take a tour of its lovely **Victorian waterfront in Onset Bay,** along West and South boulevards, which lead onto Onset Avenue and bring you to the town pier. Enormous Victorian summer cottages festooned with turrets and gables appear along this stretch, the sidewalk accented by black iron lampposts and cobblestoned sidewalks; a small park with a gazebo reaches up the hill. At the town pier is a ramshackle restaurant that is the essence of summer, painted all in white and having an outdoor deck over the water. It serves ice cream and hot dogs and is called Kenny's of Onset Bay. Right next to Kenny's on the town pier is a ticket booth, from which cruises of the Cape Cod Canal leave (see chapter 4).

Off the Beaten Path in Worcester County

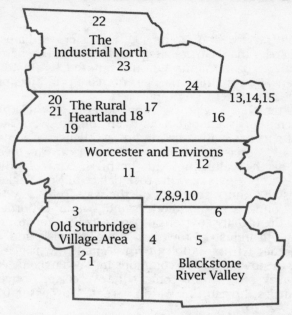

22
The
Industrial North
23

24

20   The Rural   17
21   Heartland 18
19

13,14,15

16

Worcester and Environs
12

11

7,8,9,10

3
Old Sturbridge
Village Area
2 1

6

4   5

Blackstone
River Valley

1. Bethlehem in Sturbridge
2. Saint Anne Shrine
3. Salem Cross Inn
4. Clara Barton Birthplace Museum
5. Purgatory Chasm State Reservation
6. Willard House and Clock Museum
7. Worcester Historical Museum
8. Salisbury Mansion
9. Higgins Armory Museum
10. American Sanitary Plumbing Museum
11. Moore State Park
12. Tower Hill Botanic Garden
13. Fruitlands Museums
14. Shaker Historic District
15. Holy Hill Conservation Area
16. Toy Cupboard Theatre and Museum
17. Wachusett Mountain State Reservation
18. Wachusett Meadow Wildlife Sanctuary
19. Hartman's Herb Farm
20. Petersham Craft Center
21. Fisher Museum of Forestry
22. Winchendon Historical Society
23. Gardner Heritage State Park
24. Leominster Historical Society

Worcester County

Once you travel west of Route 495, you've crossed a psychological barrier that is acutely felt by those who live here. Residents feel scorned, spurned, and ignored by Bostonians. Bostonians, in turn, think they've entered a primitive, provincial place of no interest or importance.

Worcester, New England's second-largest city, has historically been seen as a poor cousin to Boston. But Worcester is a pleasant surprise, with a handful of excellent museums and a rich past. Worcester is where the dining car was invented, as well as the Valentine and the birth control pill. The Worcester Centrum is now the rock palace of New England.

Worcester County stretches all the way from New Hampshire to Connecticut and Rhode Island. Within its borders are not only the big-city environs of Worcester but territory ranging from old industrial towns to apple orchards and wineries, together with a clutch of rural small towns featuring some of the loveliest town commons in New England.

For travel information, contact the Worcester Convention and Visitors Bureau, 33 Waldo Street, Worcester 01608; (508–753–2920).

Old Sturbridge Village Area

The high-visibility Old Sturbridge Village dominates this area, and throngs of tourists crowd it almost year-round. But right here are a number of lesser-known and interesting diversions.

Tucked away just 1 block from Old Sturbridge Village is a unique attraction that most tourists miss: **Bethlehem in Sturbridge.** This 50-foot diorama shows the people and villages of the time of Christ, almost 2,000 years ago. Following a lifelong interest, George Duquette built the diorama in his basement over thirty years. He presents a dramatic sound-and-light show with it that pilgrims come by the busload to see, especially during Christmas and Easter.

The more than 600 tiny figures include slaves at work in

the limestone quarries, Roman soldiers on horseback, women crushing grapes with their feet to make wine, and, of course, Mary and Joseph and the baby Jesus. As well, there are camels and sheep, palm trees and olive groves, tents and town squares. Much of the diorama is animated: camp fires smoke, birds fly, and horses and donkeys move. There are plants, dirt, and stones from the Holy Land, as well as water from the Jordan River, gathered on Duquette's four trips to Israel.

In the darkened theater, stars shine overhead and a narration describes the Creation and the life of Christ. Accompanying colorful photos of daily life in Israel play on a screen. The audience sits in white pews with red seats, just as in church. While the whole idea might sound tacky, it's a truly moving experience because of the sincere vision and spirit of George Duquette. Pope John Paul II blessed Duquette, and audiences have included four bishops and the wife of Augusto Pinochet, the former President of Chile.

Duquette displays some 1,000 nativity scenes from all over the world in a little museum next to the diorama. Visitors can see an Italian nativity of hand-carved alabaster, one made of cookie dough from South America, and one made of seashells from Florida. A colored-paper nativity from Germany dates back a hundred years, and a scene from Austria is handmade of crystal.

Bethlehem in Sturbridge is just off the Old Sturbridge Village entrance road from Route 20, at 72 Stallion Hill. For reservations—advised at Christmastime—call (508) 347–3013 or write P.O. Box 451, Sturbridge 01566. Performances are held at 2:00 and 7:00 P.M. at Christmastime, starting the Saturday after Thanksgiving, and at 2:00 P.M. Easter weekend; there are also 2:00 P.M. shows from July 4 to Labor Day. The museum is open daily from 10:00 A.M. to 4:00 P.M.

A winery can't get much homier than the Mellea Winery (508–943–5166), three acres of vineyards opened by Joe and Allie Compagnone in 1989. Still, just like big Napa Valley wineries, Mellea gives free tastings and tours of its two-room winery downstairs from the gift shop. Much of their equipment is hand-operated, including the bottling, corking, and capping machines.

The winery produces two red and four white wines, grown from French-American varietals. You can drink your wine at a lovely picnic area near a small pond. Mellea Winery is open from noon to 5:00 P.M. Wednesday through Sunday, Memorial Day weekend through October, and weekends in November and December. The winery, located less than twenty minutes from Old Sturbridge Village, is at 108 Old Southbridge Road, off Route 131 in Dudley.

Some believe in miracles. Their cast-off crutches and canes flank the white statue of Saint Anne at the **Saint Anne Shrine** in Sturbridge, where red and green votive candles glow in the dimness. The faithful believe a miracle took place here in 1887 when, with the help of Saint Anne, a woman parishioner was healed of dropsy. Ever since, pilgrims have flocked to the shrine in such numbers that an outdoor chapel was built for Sunday Mass.

Even if you don't believe in miracles, a visit here is well worth your while to see the museum of some sixty rare eighteenth- and nineteenth-century Russian icons. The icons feature elaborate artistry in lacquerware, gold and silver fili-gree, or mother-of-pearl. The most impressive of these exquisite and valuable pieces is a 5-foot-tall triptych in gold and silver of Christ, the Virgin, and Saint Nicholas.

Saint Anne Shrine is at 16 Church Street in the Fiskdale section of Sturbridge; call (508) 347–7338. The museum is open from 10:00 A.M. to 4:00 P.M. Monday through Friday, from 10:00 A.M. to 6:00 P.M. Saturday, and from 9:00 A.M. to 6:00 P.M. Sunday.

You know you're getting close to Old Sturbridge Village on Route 20 when you see a thick cluster of shops and restau-rants with names like "Yankee" this and "Old" that. When you're hungry, you might try The Whistling Swan, at 502 Main Street (508–347–2321), which serves an American-Continental menu in an elegant dining room and a more casual menu upstairs in a restored barn, or Crabapple's Eating & Drinking Place, on the Common, Route 131 (508–347–5559), a brightly lighted, family-style restaurant with booths and a wide-ranging menu.

A shop of a different stripe is the Oakwood Farm Christ-mas Barn (508–885–3558) on Route 31 north in Spencer, a 175-year-old barn that sells ornaments, wreaths, garlands, music boxes, and nutcrackers. It's open from early March through mid-January.

Just west of Spencer is a uniquely historical restaurant and inn, the **Salem Cross Inn.** The house was built in 1705 by a grandson of Peregrine White, the baby born on the *Mayflower* as it lay in Plymouth Harbor. The inn is richly paneled and extensively furnished with impressive collections of antiques: tin lanterns, portraits, redware, tall case clocks, and old prints, books, and maps. Come dinnertime, you can feast heartily on traditional dishes of beef, pork, chicken, seafood, fish, chowder, and Indian pudding, with meats cooked over the open hearth on a 1700s roasting jack in the fieldstone fireplace. Apple pie bakes in the 1699 brick beehive oven. In summer, an old-time "Drover's Roast" is held, offering a side of beef cooked as it used to be by drovers driving their cattle to market in Boston—over an open pit. On the 600-acre farm, hayrides and sleigh rides are part of the festivities. The Salem Cross Inn is on Route 9 in West Brookfield. Dinner reservations are strongly advised anytime and are required for hearthside dinners served on Friday nights. Call (508) 867–2345 or (508) 867–8337.

Antiques shopping galore is available at the Brimfield Flea Market and Antiques Show, held in spring, summer, and fall along Route 20. For sheer size and volume, this show is not to be beat. Shows last ten days to two weeks. Hundreds of dealers converge on the area, coming from as far as Alabama and Texas, selling everything from Hoosier cabinets to brass light fixtures. Although it takes a lot of stamina to attend this show and prices are not necessarily bargains, you should be able to find whatever you want. To learn the dates of upcoming shows, call the Information Line at (413) 245–7479.

A refreshing antidote to precious country inns is Vernalwood Bed & Breakfast in Dudley, hidden away in peace and quietude down a dirt road 8 miles from Sturbridge. Vernalwood is a hale and hearty place that speaks of old New England, an 1895 farmhouse standing on a hundred lovely and unspoiled acres. Innkeepers Van and Priscilla Van de Workeen have two large resident farm dogs, Diggy and Emily.

Despite the rustic exterior of the farmhouse, the Van de Workeens have remodeled the inside of their home in a luxuriously comfortable style, with six fireplaces, cathedral ceilings, skylights, and a greenhouse Jacuzzi. Still, they've kept some nice antique touches: One of the two guest rooms has a four-poster; the other has an antique sleigh bed with a duvet and feather bed, heavenly to sleep on.

When she can't sleep, Priscilla bakes bread. This goes into her thickly cut honey-orange French toast, just one morsel of the elaborate breakfasts she serves. For information, write the owners at RR 3, Box 375, Dudley 01570, or call (508) 943–5282. You can also book through Priscilla's reservation service, Folkstone at (800) 762–2751. Doubles cost $70 to $75.

Blackstone River Valley

If you did not hear about Lake Chargoggagoggmanchaug-gagoggchaubunagungamaugg in the fourth grade, now's the time. This is said to be the longest geographic name in the United States. It's an Indian word, translated as "You fish on your side, I fish on my side, nobody fish in the middle." For short you can call it Webster Lake, where it's located, on Route 197.

Clara Barton, founder of the American Red Cross, was born in a simple white farmhouse in North Oxford in 1821, now the **Clara Barton Birthplace Museum.** Amazingly, Clara never trained as a nurse. One story notes that she tended her bedridden little brother after he fell from the barn roof. She did not found the Red Cross until she was sixty. Before that, she was a teacher, and she was at the front lines in the Civil War. Besides nursing the soldiers and getting blankets and honey for them, she wrote their letters home, using a small wooden field desk that folded up so that it could be carried on a wagon.

The field desk is on view, as is a handmade quilt given to Clara with each of its twenty-seven blocks signed by Civil War officers. Many other family memorabilia and furnishings fill the house. The 1790 kitchen has an unusual indoor well with an oak bucket hanging from a rope. The museum is located at 68 Clara Barton Road, North Oxford; call (508) 987–5375. It's open from 11:00 A.M. to 5:00 P.M. Thursday through Sunday, April 1 to October 31, and by appointment November through March. Admission is $2.50 for adults and $1.00 for children.

A truly challenging hike can be had at **Purgatory Chasm State Reservation.** A huge ravine strewn with giant boulders, this dramatic chasm reaches down almost 80 feet. The steep, half-mile loop trail down from the parking lot takes you right through the middle of the gorge and gives your legs and lungs a real workout. Here and there, the boulders form a warren of little chambers and caves that children love to crawl into. The park also has picnic tables and a playground. Purgatory Chasm is on Purgatory Road off Route 146, about 10 miles south of Worcester; call (508) 234–3733. The chasm is closed in winter because of the danger posed by slippery rocks.

Somewhere in New England, you may have seen one of the famous clocks made by Simon Willard. Simon's three brothers, Benjamin, Ephraim, and Aaron, were all famous clockmakers, too. The brothers Willard lived and worked in a cranberry red colonial house in Grafton, now the **Willard House and Clock Museum.** To get there, you drive through acres of sheep pastures and stone walls. The house began as one room in 1718 and still has a palpable quality of being lived in. One feels oneself a guest upon entering the stooped and narrow doorway. Clocks tick amiably from every room, periodically chiming off in many voices. There are some sixty clocks made by all four brothers, the largest such collection in existence.

The brothers invented and made clocks until 1839. Simon invented the "banjo" clock, named for its shape, although Simon never called it a banjo clock. The brothers became known for their tall case clocks, what most people call grandfather clocks, many with elegant brass finials and brass-filled stop fluting. The most splendid clock is a large round wall clock that is topped with a massive gold eagle and was made for the First Church of Roxbury. There's also a musical case clock, made by Simon, that plays one of seven different tunes on the hour. Another Willard hallmark was a painted scene on the face, such as Mount Vernon or Mary and her little lamb.

The brothers' workshop is much as it was, benches strewn with tools and works, the only eighteenth-century American clock shop still in its original location. The museum is on Willard Street, a short distance from Grafton Center; call (508) 839–3500. It's open from 10:00 A.M. to 4:00 P.M. Tuesday through Saturday and from 1:00 to 5:00 P.M. Sunday. Admission is $2.00.

Just north of Grafton is Lake Quinsigamond. Here, sitting

on a lakeside deck in season, you can dine with a panoramic view of the lake, watching boaters go to and fro, at McQuale's, located at 7 Boston Turnpike in Shrewsbury (508–792–0700). The American and Italian menu includes steaks, seafood, and all-homemade desserts.

Worcester and Environs

Worcester's heritage is on view at the **Worcester Historical Museum,** at 30 Elm Street (508–753–8278). Though it's small, this museum packs a lot into its beautifully designed galleries. Holdings include many artifacts that belonged to Worcester residents in times past, such as furniture, memorabilia, clothing, artworks, and simple household items. Among the artifacts are an eighteenth-century delftware charger, a tricorn hatbox, the Lord's Prayer inscribed on a seashell, and a petrified buffalo horn brought back from the West.

Oil paintings show Worcester was astonishingly rural until the mid-nineteenth-century manufacturing boom. Patent models represent some of the many clever machines invented in Worcester: a rolling mill, twine reels, a harness motion for a loom. Around 1900, Worcester also became the country's leading producer of lunch wagons. Four custom-made lunch wagon windows are lighted to show off their rich design painted in red and white. The museum opens at 10:00 A.M. Tuesday through Saturday and at 1:00 P.M. Sunday, and it closes at 4:00 P.M. Admission is $2.00.

Stephen Salisbury was a leading citizen of Worcester, and in 1772 he built an exquisite mansion in downtown Lincoln Square, later moved to 40 Highland Street. Besides being one of the few surviving eighteenth-century houses from Worcester's Main Street, the house is so gorgeous that people love to get married here.

The **Salisbury Mansion** has serenely symmetrical Georgian lines, with beautiful matching fanlight doorways front and rear, a pillared portico, and four tall chimneys. Patterned wallpapers and carpets, as well as paint colors, have been faithfully re-created using extensive family records. These records make the mansion one of the best-documented historic houses in New England.

Downstairs, Stephen ran a "hardware" store that sold imported teas and molasses, flax, sheep's wool, chocolate, ginger, beeswax, pewter, brass, and copper. In the original kitchen hangs the large wooden store sign bearing the Salisbury logo of a samovar. House tours are given from 1:00 to 4:00 P.M. Tuesday through Sunday; admission is $2.00. For information, call the Worcester Historical Museum at (508) 753–8278. Year-round programs include vintage Christmas decorations, classical concerts, and afternoon teas.

The romance of knighthood and chivalry lives on at the **Higgins Armory Museum,** one of the best collections of medieval armor in the country. The centerpiece is the Great Hall, which feels like a castle, with its stone Gothic arches, rose-patterned stained-glass window, and cathedral ceiling. An impressive array of shining suits of armor lines the Great Hall from end to end, as do halberds and lances, hauberks, and crossbows.

A sound-and-light show re-creates all the pageantry and heraldry of a tournament, featuring two life-size knights on horseback, their lances atilt. Trumpets flare, hoofbeats gallop, and weapons clash resoundingly. It makes you think of Ivanhoe and Sir Richard the Lionhearted.

An armored knight on horseback might wear as much as ninety-five pounds of armor. It's a wonder that anyone could even walk, let alone fight, in a getup like this. Some of the armor is surprisingly beautiful, such as a sixteenth-century Italian suit made of gilded blued steel, engraved with gold floral motifs.

The several thousand pieces in the collection also include some rare items, such as a Roman gladiator's helmet and Greek Corinthian helmets from about 550 B.C. Look too for the little white dog in armor, sporting a grand red head plume. One whole floor is devoted to hands-on fun for children, including trying on armor, making brass rubbings, and dressing up as Maid Marian or King Arthur. The Higgins Armory is located at 100 Barber Avenue; call (508) 853–6015. It's open from 9:00 A.M. to 4:00 P.M. Tuesday through Friday and from noon to 4:00 P.M. weekends; it's also open Mondays in July and August. Admission is $4.00 for adults and $2.75 for senior citizens and children.

Worcester's large rainbow of ethnic groups means there are

all kinds of ethnic restaurants. Here are a couple of choices: Italian dishes at Arturo's, located at 411 Chandler Street (508–755–5640), and real home-cooked Lebanese food at El Morocco, at 100 Wall Street (508–756–7117), where the dining room looks just like a Moroccan restaurant.

What do you do with an old toilet? If you're Russell Manoog, a plumbing distributor who followed his father into the business, you save it, along with dozens of other vintage fixtures. Russell exhibits them all at his **American Sanitary Plumbing Museum,** the country's only such museum, opened in 1988.

Russell's father collected antique fixtures for sixty years. The oldest item is a section of centuries-old wooden water main, installed in Boston around 1652. An early, primitive indoor toilet looks more like an outhouse seat. By contrast, an 1891 earthenware toilet is elegantly painted with green and white floral motifs embossed with gold tracings. And an enamel hopper boasts beautiful scenes, painted in blue, of people, trees, buildings, and forests—a duplicate of a hopper at Mount Vernon. Among the museum's chamber pots is one made of white Limoges china that came from the French ocean liner *Ile de France.*

Besides toilets, there are early copper-lined and clawfoot bathtubs, lavatories, kitchen sinks, and sitz baths, along with a large collection of plumbers' tools and blowtorches. An "electric sink" invented in 1928 was the first try at a dishwasher. As part of its "Win the War" line in 1943, Kohler offered an iron kitchen sink, iron being a noncritical material. The museum is at 39 Piedmont Street. Hours are 10:00 A.M. to 2:00 P.M. Tuesday and Thursday, except July and August. Call (508) 754–9453.

If you take Route 9 west out of Worcester, it will eventually bring you to Leicester and the shores of Lake Sargent. Overlooking the lake is a wonderful restaurant that looks just like a medieval castle inside and out, complete with turrets and towers, aptly named The Castle and located at 1230 Main Street (508–892–9090). The dining room's dark wood paneling and baronial chairs smack of the Knights of the Round Table. In warm weather, there's dining on an outdoor lakeside deck. Courtly touches include a weekend harpist at dinner and complimentary roses for women. The Continental dinner menu ranges from daily game, veal, and seafood specials to chateaubriand and rack of lamb. A more casual American menu features such dishes as duck and scallops, served with contemporary flair.

In the countryside west of Worcester, Route 9 joins up with Route 56. Follow it north to Paxton and south on Route 31 to a very special state park, **Moore State Park.** This 400-acre park was a private estate in the 1930s, landscaped with thousands of rhododendrons and azaleas. A dramatic, tree-lined drive leads down past open meadows to a swift-running brook, the site of an eighteenth-century mill village. Around a sawmill and gristmill, early settlers built a tavern, one-room schoolhouse, blacksmith shop, and mill owner's house. A self-guided tour passes among the remaining buildings and the crumbling stone foundations and cellar holes of those which are gone. The weathered blacksmith shop still sits along the brook, close to a waterfall, as does the sawmill, one of the oldest standing sawmills in New England still on its original site. Call (508) 792–3969 or (508) 368–0126 for information.

"Bring plenty of cash," warn the owners of Spag's, a discount bargain basement that sells a mishmash of everything in a warehouselike building, takes no credit cards or checks, and demands you bring your own bags. Still, shopping here is an adventure, turning up jumbo-size laundry soap, toys, fishing reels, tools, appliances, shoes, and furniture, in no particular order. Spag's is just beyond the eastern city limits, on Route 9 in Shrewsbury (no phone). Look for a giant sign bearing the smiling face of the owner.

From Shrewsbury it's a short hop up Route 140 to Boylston. Here, high on a windswept hill with a breathtaking view of Mount Wachusett and the Wachusett Reservoir, is rising the most ambitious botanical garden New England has seen. The **Tower Hill Botanic Garden** is a fifty-year project of the Worcester County Horticultural Society.

Begun in the late 1980s, the botanical garden will showcase the best plants of all kinds the gardener can find that will grow in Massachusetts. There will be theme gardens of roses, fields and meadows, fruits and vegetables, wildflowers, woodlands, wetlands, winter plants, and a rock garden. Walking and nature trails will wind through the many gardens. The horti-

109

cultural society also plans a large visitor and education center, a conservatory, and an eighteenth-century-style orangery.

The two first major gardens opened in 1990, an orchard containing more than a hundred antique flavorful varieties of apples, formerly growing all over New England, and the Lawn Garden, featuring woody trees and shrubs. Above the Lawn Garden a bluestone terrace set with urns steps up to an eighteenth-century white farmhouse that serves both as society headquarters and as classroom space for all kinds of plant workshops.

The gardens are at 30 Tower Hill Road; call (508) 869–6111. Hours are from 9:00 A.M. to 5:00 P.M. Monday through Friday and from 10:00 A.M. to 5:00 P.M. weekends except in winter.

The Rural Heartland

North of Worcester, you'll find one small town after another, spread across the whole county from Harvard, near Route 495, all the way to the Quabbin Reservoir. This is some of the nicest territory to explore in Worcester County.

Making your way through apple orchards on Route 110, you'll come to signs for **Fruitlands Museums,** a collection of four small museums that are little-known gems. Set high on rolling green hills with a sweeping view of Mount Wachusett, the museums are surrounded by woods with nature trails. Down the hill stands the red colonial farmhouse where Bronson Alcott and like-minded others tried out their transcendentalist dream, thinking hard while the women tended the house and crops. Plain and primitively furnished, the Alcott House is pervaded by the spiritual feelings of its past occupants. The 1790s Shaker House was used as an office by the Shaker community in Harvard. It is filled with exhibits of Shaker handicrafts and industries, such as growing seeds and herbs. There's also a chair that belonged to Mother Ann, the sect's founder, who lived briefly in Harvard. The American Indian Museum holds countless decorated shields, clothing, baskets, and pottery. Finally, an ivied brick building houses the Picture Gallery, where you can see primitive portraits of children done by itinerant artists, as well as landscape paintings by Hudson River School artists.

Even if you don't tour the museums, the grounds are a wonderful place for picnicking. In summer, there are old-fashioned bandstand concerts on the lawn. The Museum Shop has some unusual, quality handicrafts. There's also a lovely tearoom enhanced by a white lattice doorway and an outdoor patio. The tearoom serves light lunches, snacks, and afternoon tea with pastries and desserts. The museums, at 102 Prospect Hill Road off Route 110 in Harvard, are open from 10:00 A.M. to 5:00 P.M. Tuesday through Sunday from mid-May through mid-October. Admission is $5.00 for adults and $1.00 for children. Call (508) 456–3924.

You can see some of the Shaker houses built by Harvard's Shaker community on Shaker Road, in the **Shaker Historic District.** These plain but attractive clapboard houses are painted in pastel colors and complemented by stone stairs, barns, and tall pines. Some other Shaker land has been set aside as the **Holy Hill Conservation Area,** on South Shaker Road, just off Shaker Road. The sanctuary gets its name from a Shaker holy hill, where religious services were held out-doors. The worship area, sometimes called "the dancing ground," is ½ mile up a trail. The grounds also include a stone bridge, a Shaker barn foundation, and a Shaker cemetery. For information, call the Harvard town clerk at (508) 456–3607. A trail guide is available at Town Hall on the town common.

For more than fifty years, puppet shows of the most loved of children's stories have been held at the **Toy Cupboard Theatre and Museum** in South Lancaster. "Puss in Boots," "The Three Bears," "Little Red Riding Hood," "Hansel and Gre-tel," "The Frog Prince"—the list of classics goes on and on. The man behind the strings is Homer Hosmer, whose one-man show began in the summer of 1941. Grandchildren of his first audiences now come. The work is a labor of love: Hosmer charges only 90 cents admission. The show goes on in a tiny theater hardly bigger than a toy box.

Hosmer also has a collection of memorabilia surrounding "The Remarkable Story of Chicken Little" ("The sky is falling! The sky is falling!") in a museum next door, where author John Greene Chandler once lived. Chandler was Hosmer's great-grand-uncle. The theater is at 57 East George Hill Road, just off Main Street. Call ahead (508–365–9519) for perfor-mance times.

Continuing west from Lancaster, you'll come to Princeton, a nineteenth-century summer resort with many hotels. There was even a three-story hotel on top of Wachusett Mountain. Today there's a park, **Wachusett Mountain State Reservation** (508–464–2987), with 20 miles of hiking trails and alpine and cross-country skiing. The visitor center is a cozy refuge for hikers, with a huge four-sided fieldstone fireplace. Views from the top are spectacular: Boston to the east and the Berkshire hills to the west. Wachusett is also a great place for seeing hawks, ospreys, falcons, and eagles, because it's along the migration route of these raptors.

More outdoor pleasures await at **Wachusett Meadow Wildlife Sanctuary,** a Massachusetts Audubon property. Though there isn't much farmland left in Massachusetts, you can see a traditional farm landscape here. The farmland is habitat for bobolink, whose numbers have declined along with farm acreage. A nature trail passes through a red maple swamp over a boardwalk with observation platforms for viewing the special plants and animals that live here. Another highlight is the Crocker Maple, one of the country's largest and more than 300 years old. Though its ancient, gnarled limbs look as if they should spread next to a haunted house, the maple is an impressive sight, especially when its leaves are aflame with color in autumn. Wachusett Meadow is also a good place for snowshoeing. To get to the sanctuary, follow Route 62 ¾ mile west and turn right at the Massachusetts Audubon sign. Admission for adults is $3.00; for children, $2.00. For information, call (508) 464–2712.

Princeton has some excellent restaurants. A quiet gourmet dinner in the countryside is a hallmark of the Harrington Farm Country Inn. This mountainside farm was built on the western slope of Wachusett Mountain in 1763 and still has hand-painted stenciling on its walls. It's surrounded by thousands of acres of protected land ideal for hiking, berry picking, and cross-country skiing. In keeping with its setting, the restaurant's menu gives a country flair to such nouvelle American dishes as grilled pheasant with rosemary, roasted tenderloin with candied shallots, roast pork loin with sautéed apples, and occasional quail and venison entrees. To take advantage of the freshest seasonal ingredients, the menu changes weekly. The restaurant is closed Mondays and Tuesdays. The seven guest rooms (doubles, $58–$100) are furnished with original farm antiques. The inn is at 178 Westminster Road; call (508) 464–5600 or (800) 736–3276.

Although the town of Barre, reached via Route 62, has a pretty town common and lots of shops, a more interesting stop is the family-owned **Hartman's Herb Farm,** which sells one of the most extensive selections of herbs you'll ever see. Its catalog lists twenty kinds of thyme, seventeen kinds of mint, and thirteen kinds of basil. Like Yosemite, the farm sprang back after a massive fire in 1989 that claimed the shop and house. But everything grows greener now, say the Hartmans. The cluster of farm buildings commands a rustic setting down a narrow blacktop road. From the new shop's beamed ceiling hang tied bundles of yellow, pink, and purple flowers and of dried herbs, all giving forth an exquisite redolence. The shop also sells plants and garden accessories, books on herbs, soup and salad herbs, herb dips, herb teas, and such handmade crafts as dried flower arrangements and wreaths, flower-decorated straw hats, raffia dolls, and cornhusk angels. On your visit, don't overlook the farm's resident pig, goats, sheep, rabbits, chickens, ducks, cats, and dog. The farm is particularly resplendent and fragrant at Christmastime, when mulled cider is served. To get to the farm, go west on Routes 122 and 32 and turn left onto Old Dana Road at the heart-shaped green sign. Call (508) 355–2015 for information.

The town of Petersham, too, has a picturesque common, complete with bandstand and Greek Revival mansions. The common is surrounded by interesting shops. A short hop from the common on North Main Street, the **Petersham Craft Center** offers a wide variety of crafts and art. The galleries in this more-than-seventy-year-old center housed in an antique white farmhouse have a homey, community feeling. Their offerings range from watercolors, blue-and-white flowered pottery, and heart-shaped, hand-forged iron hooks to linens, wooden toys, clothing, cotton rugs, and jewelry. The center is open from 11:30 A.M. to 4:00 P.M. daily except Monday. Directly opposite the common, the Country Store (508–724–3245) stands behind tall white pillars and offers such traditional products as maple syrup and cheddar cheese. A cozy, postage-stamp-size dining room in back serves sandwiches, soups, and chili and features enormous glass jars of homemade cookies.

Unknown to many is the fact that Harvard University has owned land in Petersham since 1907, for the purpose of forestry research. In 1941, a museum opened in the Harvard Forest, the **Fisher Museum of Forestry,** designed to interpret the history of New England forests. The museum is dark inside, to better show the lighted windows housing twenty-three unique dioramas. A preliminary color slide show gives background about the dioramas and showcases some beautifully artistic shots of tree canopies and forest plants.

As you go around the room, each diorama shows a particular phase of history in New England's forests, starting with a dense primeval forest of 1700 and moving on through farming, reforestation, and clear-cutting. Other dioramas portray forestry management techniques, erosion, wildlife habitat, and forest fire devastation.

Despite the dioramas' teaching intent, they are rare jewels whose like will never again be created. Hours of hand labor went into each diorama, and they are filled with purely artistic touches, such as people and vehicles, animals and birds. The trees and branches look so natural that you'd swear they were real. But even the tiniest pine needles are made of copper. One diorama looks just like a painting, of a scenic spot among the trees on Harvard Pond, aflame with the reds and oranges of sunset.

The Harvard Forest also has nature trails and cross-country ski trails—wonderfully uncrowded spots. The forest and museum are on Route 32; call (508) 724–3302. Museum hours are from 9:00 A.M. to 5:00 P.M. weekdays and from noon to 4:00 P.M. Saturdays, May to October.

The Industrial North

By 1914, the town of Winchendon made so many toys that it became known as "Toy Town," and mail would arrive addressed simply to Toy Town. Named after its founder, Winchendon's Morton E. Converse Company was the largest toy manufacturer in the country and sent wooden rocking horses all over the world. Memorabilia surrounding this hey-

Toy Town Horse, Winchendon

day are exhibited at the **Winchendon Historical Society,** in the basement of the library at 50 Pleasant Street (call 508–297–0412 for an appointment). The glass cases in the musty basement are crammed with Converse toys: dollhouses, toy trunks, drums, tea sets. Other toymakers followed on the heels of Converse's success.

Eventually, visitors to Toy Town numbered so many that Converse built a resort called the Toy Town Tavern, about which there's a scrapbook. The historical society's collection is wide-ranging and also includes artifacts from the revolutionary war, the Civil War, and World War II; eighteenth-century pewter; antique tools; clothing; portraits; and household goods. There's also a case of pre-Columbian pottery that Converse collected in Peru. A proud symbol of Toy Town, a 12-foot rocking horse stands under a canopy on Route 12, 2 blocks north of the library—a copy of the 1914 original, made as a parade float to celebrate the company's 150th anniversary.

As you drive down Elm Street in Gardner, you'll come upon a giant wooden ladder-back chair, so tall that it may remind you of Lily Tomlin's comedy prop for her routine about a little girl in a giant rocker. Townspeople joke that when the wood deteriorated, the chair was rebuilt bigger to maintain its Guinness world record as the world's largest chair. The two-story-high chair symbolizes Gardner's heritage as "Chair City," a large manufacturing city making many kinds of chairs.

The story of this heritage is outlined at **Gardner Heritage State Park.** One man, James Comee, began making chairs by hand at his Pearl Street home in 1805. The apprentices he trained went on to open their own companies. A century later, there were almost forty chair companies in Gardner, making more than four million chairs a year. Gardner still makes chairs today.

A video details the craft of chairmaking, and on display are locally made chairs of bentwood, rush, rattan, wicker, and pressed-back oak, as well as Windsor, side, bedroom, ladder-back, and hand-painted and stenciled chairs. There's also an exhibit detailing Gardner's silversmithing history. The park is at 26 Lake Street; call (508) 630–1497 or (508) 632–2099 (recording). Saturdays and weekdays (except Thursdays), the park is open from 9:00 A.M. to 4:30 P.M., as well as from noon to 4:30 P.M. Sunday. Winter hours change.

Chairmaker James Comee's house, at 162 Pearl St., is now the Hawke Bed & Breakfast (508–632–5909). Innkeeper Nancy Hawke has assembled a scrapbook on the house's history. The colonial white farmhouse was probably built around the late 1700s and now has black shutters and a gingerbread porch. Her guest rooms (doubles, $55) are simply decorated with braided rugs and flowered spreads, and the bath is shared. Breakfast is a no-nonsense affair of expertly cooked eggs or pancakes.

Another legacy of the chairmaking heritage is the many furniture factory outlets in Gardner, Winchendon, and Templeton, great places to find bargain furniture. For a map and brochure listing them, contact the Worcester County Convention and Visitors Bureau (see pg. 100).

At 102 Main Street in Gardner is a vintage diner in mint condition, the Blue Moon Diner (508–632–4333). Built by the Worcester Lunch Car Company in 1948, the diner has a handsome blue-and-cream exterior, oak-trimmed booths with blue leather seats, and the original art deco, steel diner's clock. The Italian owner, a former policeman who loves people, makes the rounds of the counter stools, booths, and tables to chat and joke with customers. Besides breakfasts of home fries, eggs, and fresh fruit pancakes, the diner has blackboard specials, such as meatloaf and pork pie, and homemade soups and pies.

Nineteenth-century novels are full of references to women pinning their long upswept hair in place with ornamental hair combs. Such combs have largely disappeared nowadays, but the **Leominster Historical Society** has the largest haircomb collection in the country. Once home to a hair-comb factory, Leominster was known as "Comb City of the World."

Hundreds of hair combs fill two whole walls. It's hard to believe they came in so many different styles. Some are 6 inches high or more, carved of tortoise shell with scrolled, floral designs. Others are made of silver and filigreed in minute detail. And still others are made in the shapes of butterflies or dragonflies and studded with rhinestones or pearls. There's an ivory comb too, cut with the design of a fire-breathing dragon, that probably hails from China or India.

Other exhibits detail the plastics industry in Leominster, combmaking machinery, and the story of Johnny Appleseed, who was born here. While many know Johnny Appleseed only as a folk hero, he was a skilled nurseryman who distributed thousands of apple trees to settlers and started many nurseries throughout the Midwest. The historical society museum is at 17 School Street (508–537–5424) and is open from 9:00 A.M. to 2:00 P.M. Monday through Thursday or by appointment.

Off the Beaten Path in the Pioneer Valley

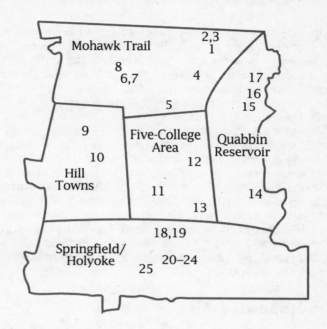

Mohawk Trail

2,3
1

8
6,7

4

17
16
15

5

9

10

Hill
Towns

Five-College
Area

12

Quabbin
Reservoir

11

14

13

18,19

Springfield/
Holyoke

25

20–24

1. *Quinnetukut II*
2. Stearns Houses
3. Northfield Country House
4. Turners Falls Fishway
5. Historic Deerfield
6. Bridge of Flowers
7. Glacial Potholes
8. Gould's Maple Farm
9. William Cullen Bryant
   Homestead
10. Chesterfield Gorge
11. Lyman Plant House
12. Emily Dickinson
    Homestead
13. Nash Dinosaur Land
14. Quabbin Reservoir

15. Hamilton Orchards
16. Swift River Valley
    Historical Society
17. Orange Historical Society
18. Holyoke Heritage
    State Park
19. Wistariahurst Museum
20. Springfield Museum
    Quadrangle
21. McKnight District
22. Mattoon Street
23. The Student Prince and
    Fort Restaurant
24. Springfield Armory
    National Historic Site
25. Storrowton Village Museum

The Pioneer Valley

No one outside the Pioneer Valley seems to know where it is. The Pioneer Valley is actually the Connecticut River Valley, and follows its course the whole length of the state.

In its distance from Boston, this may as well be another country. Residents know that Bostonians can't think of a good reason to come here. People here say "grinders" and "soda" instead of the Bostonian "submarines" and "tonic" and, unlike the Kennedys, pronounce their "r's."

Still, it's hard to find another region in this state more markedly diverse. There's farmland here so isolated you wonder if anyone lives there. There are the large industrial cities of Springfield and Holyoke, ethnic rainbows. A centuries-old tradition of craftsmanship has drawn some 1,500 artists and craftspeople to live here. Five of the state's best-known colleges are clustered here, and their thousands of students have kept the 1960s alive like another Cambridge or Berkeley. For this unique blend of outlooks, the region is also nicknamed "the Happy Valley."

The Mohawk Trail

The Mohawk Trail (Route 2), originally an Indian footpath, today stretches 63 miles from Millers Falls to the New York border. It's a scenic delight to drive, passing through miles of farmland, apple orchards, and maple sugar houses. Because of its brilliant fall foliage display, it's a popular tourist path for leaf-peeping and is often crowded in the fall. The first part of the Mohawk Trail passes through Franklin County in the northern part of the Pioneer Valley.

For travel information on the Mohawk Trail and Franklin County areas, contact the Franklin County Chamber of Commerce, P.O. Box 790, 395 Main Street, Greenfield 01302; (413) 773–5463.

Despite the bumper-to-bumper traffic on the Mohawk Trail in the fall, lots of little nooks and crannies are tucked away to explore. The easiest way to explore them is to head west from Millers Falls on Route 2, taking time out for a few detours.

One of the most worthwhile detours is up Route 63 to Northfield. From Route 63, turn off at the Northfield Mountain Recreation and Environmental Center, established by Northeast Utilities. A visitor center holds interesting exhibits on ice harvesting and logging, as well as explaining the operation of the company's hydroelectric plant. You'll find some of the area's best cross-country skiing on Northfield Mountain trails; also here are a picnic area, campgrounds, and nature trails.

But the highlight of a visit here is a scenic 12-mile ride along the Connecticut River on the ***Quinnetukut II,*** an openair riverboat with wooden benches. The ride is splendid on a sunny day, with the sunlight flashing on the waves and the breeze in your face. The wide expanse of river is flanked by unbroken green forests of pine and hardwoods, turning to rock cliffs imprinted with low-growing plants and mosses and, later, to marsh grasses. You pass under the French King Bridge, a graceful iron structure spanning 750 feet, built in 1932. You might spot a bald eagle among the many migratory birds and will certainly see geese and ducks. For information, contact Northeast Utilities, RR 2, Box 177, Northfield 01360; (413) 659–3714. The boat ride costs $6.00 for adults and $2.50 for children.

Downtown Northfield, sprawled out along Route 63, is a pleasant village whose wide Main Street has an architectural treasure trove called the **Stearns Houses.** Fifteen whiteclapboarded houses were built by two generations of Stearns carpenters over a hundred years, starting in 1802. Their architectural grace and sophistication are unusual in such a small town: Greek columns, leaded glass, and fan-shaped designs carved into the wood around the windows. At one time, one of the Stearnses worked for Charles Bulfinch and Asher Benjamin.

The Stearns family also built some of the campus of nearby Northfield–Mount Hermon School for boys, a prestigious school founded by evangelist Dwight Moody, who ran summer religious conferences in Northfield. A follower of Moody's built an extravagantly ornate house out in the woods to stay in only two weeks each summer during the meetings.

The house is now the **Northfield Country House** bed-and-breakfast inn. A dirt road shaded by towering pines imparts an otherworldly quality of peace and tranquillity to this nineteenth-century manor. The large house is handsome and comfortable inside and out. The outside is fronted by rough stone columns and hundred-year-old hydrangeas with startlingly huge white blossoms. Inside are exquisitely carved cherrywood moldings and china closets, as well as a 12-foot fieldstone hearth. Rooms are decorated with floral wallpapers, iron and brass bedsteads, and antiques. Some have fireplaces. Innkeeper Andrea Dale will be happy to point you to the best local antiques shops and to arrange a tour of the Stearns Houses. Write the inn at School Street, Northfield 01360, or call (413) 498–2692.

One of Andrea's favorite antiques shops is Northfield Antiques (413–498–5825), at 37 Main Street. It's tough to move around in this big old barn because it's so stuffed with antique tools, collectibles, and furniture.

If you rode on the *Quinnetukut II,* you probably noticed a dam along the river. Just below the dam is the **Turners Falls Fishway** (413–659–3714), where fish ladders built by Northeast Utilities help anadromous fish make it back upriver to spawn. (Anadromous fish are fish born in fresh water that swim downstream to feed and grow in the ocean before returning upstream to reproduce; examples are shad and salmon.) The fish have been in great decline on the Connecticut River, and the fish ladders are helping to increase the population.

From mid-May through mid-June, you can watch the fish through viewing windows as they fight the current on their way upriver to spawn, from 9:00 A.M. to 5:00 P.M. Wednesday through Sunday. Along the riverbank is a small, grassy picnic area with a serene view of the river. You might pick up a lunch at the Shady Glen Diner, at 7 Avenue A in downtown Turners Falls (413–863–9636).

Another excellent lunch spot close by on Route 2 is the Red Apple tearoom (413–863–2181) in Gill, which serves breakfast, lunch, and afternoon tea. It's in a little red house built in 1736 that once served Connecticut River boatmen as a tavern during logging days. The intimate dining rooms have been made sumptuous with Victorian and Federal motifs, replete with gilded mirrors, lace curtains, shelves of painted china tea sets, and portraits of gowned ladies. Lunch offers tidy little sandwiches and such homemade desserts as apricot-pineapple pie with a sugared crust, served warm from the oven. Tea is served from 3:00 to 5:00 P.M. A Christmas shop in the back sells Christmas ornaments, dried wreaths and flowers, and snow villages.

Another handy place to stay when touring the Mohawk Trail area is The Brandt House B & B, a stately blue-and-white Victorian set high on a hill. This rambling house has all sorts of rooms, from a billiards room and a living room opening into a dining room to a wonderful sun-room retreat with white sofas on the second floor. Guest rooms, some with private baths, feature high ceilings, jewel-like colors of mauve and green, fresh flowers, and lots of lace. Both innkeeper Phoebe Brandt and her husband, George, are gourmet cooks. Their breakfasts might offer such delicacies as homemade lemon or pumpkin bread, or French toast marinated in orange juice and Grand Marnier. It's quiet at night, with only the katydids for company. Write the establishment at 29 Highland Avenue, Greenfield 01301, or call (413–773–8184).

For some moderately priced food that's plain but good, stop in at Turnbull's Restaurant at the Route 2 and I–91 rotary in Greenfield (413–773–8203). The fare includes sandwiches, fish, steaks, and salads in a country setting.

From Greenfield it's just a hop, skip, and a jump down I–91 to **Historic Deerfield** (413–774–5581). Though this is a well-known tourist attraction, it's still a special place to visit. The faithfulness and purity of its surroundings give a powerful sense of the past. The original Deerfield was a farming community founded in 1669. Twelve of its eighteenth- and nineteenth-century houses have been preserved and opened as house museums. The clapboarded houses with mullioned windows and imposing Connecticut Valley doors stand serenely in oases of green lawns, neatly contained by wooden fences. When you look out in the distance, you see nothing but cornfields, just as it was centuries ago. Cars look out of place driving along the main street, called simply "The Street," where no trace of modernity intrudes. Families still live cheek by jowl with the house museums on The Street and still use the old post office and church.

Each house offers its own treasures, remarkable collections of American decorative arts. The Stebbins House, the first

Historic Deerfield

brick house built in the county, features a carved freestanding staircase, painted ceiling garlands, Chinese export porcelain, tasseled swag draperies, and hand-painted French murals showing the voyages of Captain Cook in the Sandwich Islands. Another house holds dozens of glass cases full of exquisitely repouséed and engraved silver, from the seventeenth century on up. Besides coffee pots and candlesticks, there's a pagoda-shaped, filigreed epergne so beautiful it could be a piece of sculpture.

Historic Deerfield also includes a restored inn, the Deerfield Inn (413–774–5587), and a museum shop that sells some nice reproductions, books, and handicrafts. Historic Deerfield is open daily from 9:30 A.M. to 4:30 P.M. A ticket to all twelve houses costs $7.50.

Another short detour off the Mohawk Trail up Routes 5 and 10 will bring you to an excellent restaurant in Bernardston, the Four Leaf Clover Restaurant (413–648–9514). A country place full of good cheer, this little restaurant, founded in 1949, has wooden booths and excellently priced homemade food. Lunches feature generous hot and cold sandwiches, as well as salads. At dinner, you can get chicken potpie, seafood, or veal cutlets, among the other classic dishes. Top it all off with homemade puddings and pies or a sundae. Be prepared to wait in line on a Saturday night.

Head west again from Greenfield and you'll come to the village of Shelburne Falls, where you could easily spend a whole day or several. The village is blessed with really nice shops, galleries, and restaurants, along with two strikingly unusual attractions. The first is the **Bridge of Flowers,** a graceful, five-arch span over the Deerfield River. Three seasons of the year beautiful blooming plants line both sides of this old 1920s trolley bridge, making it a wonderful spot for a stroll. The local women's club planted it with more than 500 species, including crocuses and other spring bulbs, chrysanthemums, delphinium, foxglove, and wisteria. It's also nice to look at from the riverbanks, and the bridge is lighted at night.

At the end of the bridge is a small, laid-back restaurant— the kind where you'll still find a folksinger on a Sunday night—called Marty's Riverside Restaurant & Bakery (413–625–2570). From its wide windows, you have a good view of the river and the Bridge of Flowers. The cafe menu ranges from homemade soups and vegetarian dishes to Mexican and Szechuan, in addition to smashing baked desserts, such as blueberry *genoise* and Mexican icebox cookies.

Diagonally across the street from Marty's is a great place to stock up on picnic fixings: McCusker's Market & Deli (413–625–9411). Freshly made pasta and tabouli salads are specialties, as are gourmet coffees and teas and homemade ice cream.

The other truly unusual sight in Shelburne Falls is the **Glacial Potholes.** Glacial potholes are round holes carved into stone millions of years ago by the glacial action of water swirling rocks along the ground. Besides being an interesting natural phenomenon, Shelburne Falls's glacial potholes make great swimming holes. The potholes vary from a few inches to almost 40 feet in diameter, scattered along the riverbed with little waterfalls here and there. The rock surface is a moonscape of smooth curves, perfect for sunning. To get to the potholes, walk down the steps behind Mole Hollow Candles on Deerfield Avenue.

Before leaving Shelburne Falls, be sure to stop into the Salmon Falls Artisans Showroom (413–625–9833), 1 block from the Bridge of Flowers, on Ashfield Street. It's housed in an old three-story granary that nicely showcases the high-quality work of more than a hundred regional artists and craftspeople. Wares include paintings, jewelry, pottery, weaving, sculpture, and furniture. The showroom is open daily May through December and closed Mondays in winter.

As you travel the Mohawk Trail, you'll see lots of signs for maple sugar farms. One of the best to visit is **Gould's Maple Farm** (413–625–6170), 7 miles west of I–91. Gould's has been making maple syrup for more than thirty years and lets visitors watch each spring. A shed behind the 1827 barn holds the old-fashioned, wood-fired evaporators that boil down the maple sap in March. You can have "sugar on snow," a traditional New England treat, and buy homemade syrup and maple sugar candy. The biggest treat, though, is breakfast in the Gould Sugar House. The country-style dining room could not be more rustic, with oxbows hanging from the rafters, wooden picnic tables covered with red-and-white-checkered tablecoths, an old wood stove, and the smell of maple syrup hanging warmly in the air. Feast on homemade pancakes, corn fritters, and waffles, all served with the sweet golden liquid. Large windows offer spectacular vistas of the surrounding forests. Gould's is open daily from March 1 through October, except for the month of April.

The last noteworthy detour off the Mohawk Trail is the road to Colrain, marked by a green sign just past the Mohawk Orchards. This scenic drive takes you through apple orchards so thick with fruit in autumn that you can smell the apples hanging on the trees. The road passes through bucolic meadows, fields of goldenrod, corn patches, and pine-forested ridges. Then it goes through the center of Colrain, not much more than a church, post office, and hall. A little later it brings you to a tiny covered bridge on Lyonsville Road, one of only four original nineteenth-century covered bridges left in Massachusetts. Restoration of the bridge was begun in 1990, using hundred-year-old methods—teams of pulling oxen hauled it from its footings.

The Hill Towns

Driving through the "hill towns" of Franklin County is pure pleasure. These tiny villages are some of the most rural and traditional in all of New England. In particular, take Route 112 south from Route 9 through the Worthingtons: Worthington Corners, Worthington Center, and South Worthington. As it heads south from Route 9, Route 112 is barely one lane wide and is lined with thick-trunked trees that grow right out to the edge of the road. Sheep graze, and farmers harrow their fields. You'll pass a pick-your-own blueberry farm, Cumworth Farm. At Worthington Corners there's an old-fashioned general store, the Worthington Corners Grocery.

A turnoff from Route 112 leads you to the **William Cullen Bryant Homestead** (413–634–2244) in Cummington, boyhood and country home of the famous poet and *New York Post* editor. This home was a splendid retreat for Bryant, and he derived much inspiration for his poetry here. Handsome, tall maples line the long drive up to the rambling, twenty-three-room white house with open-air porches and gambrel roof. The house commands superb views of the countryside and is at such a high remove that it seems to float in its own green sea. In Bryant's day, the homestead was very much a working farm, with productive orchards and fields. The house is filled with Bryant's belongings and with souvenirs of his travels around the world. Among them are his Empire maple canopied four-poster bed, a fit bed for a poet. His straw hat for berry picking still rests on a corner of his oak desk in the study, which has a view of the Hampshire Hills in the distance. The Bryant Homestead is open from 1:00 to 5:00 P.M. Sunday to Friday in summer and only on weekends after Labor Day until Columbus Day. Admission is $2.00 for adults and $1.25 for children.

Every summer, the hill towns come alive with the sound of music at the Sevenars Music Festival in Worthington. This unique classical festival is named after a family of seven whose names all begin with "R." As a family affair, the concerts are intimate and friendly. Yet the family has won much acclaim performing at major concert halls around the world and invites many distinguished guest performers during the season. For information, call (413) 238–5854.

The most rugged spot in the hill towns is **Chesterfield Gorge.** A deep canyon carved into sheer granite cliffs, the gorge courses with tumbling white water. Looking down into its swirling depths is a dizzying experience. You can also see the crumbling stone remnants of a bridge over the gorge, built in 1739, a part of the Boston to Albany Post Road. Thick forests of pine and hemlock shelter picnic tables here and there. The gorge is a Trustees of Reservation property; call (413) 298–3239 for information.

The Five-College Area

Naturally enough, there are five college campuses here: Mount Holyoke, Smith, Hampshire, Amherst, and the University of Massachusetts. The campuses all have interesting museums, and the lively student life means there are plenty of restaurants and shops.

One of the more intriguing shops is Rumplestiltskin Architectural Antiques on Route 9 in Haydenville (413–268–7604). This is where old parts of buildings go to be reincarnated in somebody else's house. There's barely room to walk around the old doors, pillars, shutters, and banisters, as well as clawfoot bathtubs, brass light fixtures, and train station benches. How about picking something up for the parlor?

A favored student eatery, because it's so cheap, is the Miss Florence Diner on North Main Street (Route 9) in Florence. This is an authentic vintage diner, with bright yellow sides lettered in red art deco, green awnings, and glass block corners. Yankee pot roast, meatloaf, or baked stuffed peppers usually won't set you back much more than $5.00.

While all the campuses have their attractions, one of the nicest places to visit is the **Lyman Plant House** at Smith College in Northampton. It gives you a real lift no matter what the season to walk into these labyrinthine greenhouses and smell the potting soil and growing things. Besides scads of common plants like begonias and African violets, the thirteen greenhouses hold tropical plants from Africa, cacti from the Peruvian desert, and tree ferns from Tasmania—3,500 species in all. Outdoor gardens and an arboretum surround the 1890s greenhouses. They're open daily from 8:00 A.M. to 4:15 P.M.; call (413) 584–2700.

Northampton is a busy town that's chockablock with shops and restaurants, so many that it's hard to choose among them. For good food at reasonable prices, you might try the Italian fare at Spoleto, located at 12 Crafts Avenue (413–586–6313); the baked goods and sandwiches at Curtis & Schwartz, at 116 Main Street (413–586–3278); or vegetarian and natural foods at Paul and Elizabeth's, in Thorne's Market, 150 Main Street (413–584–4832), a popular place whose decor features earth colors and wood tables.

Thorne's Market complex at 150 Main Street is also a fine place to shop. It's a five-story vintage department store that was spiffed up into new and contemporary boutiques, whose wares include books, records, crafts, linens, women's and children's clothing, and toys.

Calvin Coolidge was an Amherst grad and lived many years in Northampton, up until his death in 1933. Before becoming president, he practiced law and served as mayor and governor. A collection of his personal mementos, family photos, and souvenirs of office is exhibited in the Calvin Coolidge Memorial Room in the Forbes Library (413–584–6037). Amid these family memorabilia, "Silent Cal" seems a little more human. Although the official White House oil portraits of Coolidge and his wife hang on the wall, there are also many black-and-white photos of the Coolidges, who had two sons, one of whom died a premature death. Also in the collection is a full Indian feather headdress that a descendant of Sitting Bull gave to Coolidge in Black Hills, South Dakota, where Coolidge kept a summer White House. Although many constituents thought he looked pretty funny in the headdress, Coolidge was not too proud to be photographed wearing it. The library is located at 20 West Street; the memorial room is open from 9:00 A.M. to 5:00 P.M. Monday through Friday.

The Arcadia Nature Center and Wildlife Sanctuary is a pleasant place to spend a morning or an afternoon. Located on an ancient oxbow of the Connecticut River, it has trails leading through floodplain forest, meadowland, and a marsh, with an observation tower overlooking it. All kinds of programs are offered, including canoe excursions on the Connecticut River, hawk watches, and wildflower walks. The sanctuary is located at 127 Combs Road, in Easthampton. Admission is $3.00 for adults and $2.00 for children. Call (413) 584–3009.

"Because I could not stop for Death, / He kindly stopped for me; / The carriage held but just ourselves / And Immortality." These lines were written by "the Belle of Amherst"—poet Emily Dickinson, who spent her whole life here. At the **Emily Dickinson Homestead**, you can see where she lived and worked. The brick mansion with white trim is so heavily shaded by thick-growing trees that it looks as secretive as Emily herself. The poet lived a strange, reclusive life, spending most of her time at home. In her later years she dressed all in white and never left the house. Still, she wrote powerfully of life and death, love and nature. Unknown and virtually unpublished in her lifetime, she became one of America's most famous poets only after her death.

Although most of the house is an Amherst College faculty home, you can see several rooms. In the poet's spare, simple bedroom are the sleigh bed she slept in and one of the white dresses she wore. The house, located at 280 Main Street, is open from 1:30 to 3:45 P.M. Wednesdays and Saturdays in March and April and from November through December 15; it's also open the same hours Wednesday through Saturday from May through October. Reservations are advised. Call (413) 542–8161. Admission is $3.00.

The world's only "dinosaur quarry," **Nash Dinosaur Land,** is in South Hadley. Although scientists recoil in horror at the idea, entrepreneur Carlton Nash has made a fifty-year business of selling real, 200-million-year-old dinosaur tracks found here by a local farmer in 1802. Nash has sold the tracks to such celebrities as the late General George S. Patton, at prices varying according to size and rarity, up to thousands of dollars. What do you do with dinosaur tracks? Use them as paperweights, edge your pool or garden with them, keep them as conversation pieces. Nash Dinosaur Land is on Route 116; call (413) 467–9566. The quarry and the museum are closed between Christmas and March.

The Quabbin Reservoir

If you head east out of Amherst on Route 9, the road will bring you to the **Quabbin Reservoir,** a 55,000-acre watershed that supplies greater Boston's drinking water. This vast tract also offers splendid recreation: fishing, hiking from most of its fifty-two gates, biking, and picnicking. There's a spectacular array of wildlife in its thick woods, from white-tailed deer and beaver to wild turkeys and hawks. The Quabbin is also the best place in Massachusetts to see bald eagles, which were reestablished here as a nesting species in the state, as were wild loons.

A sign on Route 9 marks Quabbin Park, a small peninsula of the reservoir that has a lookout tower, a dam, and a visitor center (413–323–7221). In the visitor center, a colored board shows the serpentine journey the water takes from the Quabbin to Boston. To create the reservoir, four towns in the Swift River Valley were flooded in 1939; on display are aerial photos taken of those towns in 1930, before they were obliterated. A video presents oral histories of former town residents. (Mementos from the four towns are preserved at the Swift River Valley Historical Society up the road a piece, which is discussed later in this chapter). The Quabbin Park Cemetery is where all the graves of the Swift River Valley were reinterred, some dating back to colonial times. The visitor center also has trail maps, as well as books and brochures on the Quabbin. Located at 485 Ware Road in Belchertown, the visitor center is open from 8:30 A.M. to 4:30 P.M. weekdays and from 9:00 A.M. to 5:00 P.M. weekends.

Route 9 intersects with Route 202, which winds around the western half of the reservoir and offers several interesting stops along the way.

Deeply hidden away in the tiny town of Leverett, just west of Route 202, is Leverett Crafts & Arts, a small gallery housed in a renovated 1875 box factory. Some dozen artists display weaving, pottery, sculpture, furniture, glass, jewelry, fiber, baskets, candles, handmade cards, toys, photographs, and paintings. Several times a year, they hold new gallery exhibitions. The gallery is on Montague Road and is open from noon to 5:00 P.M. weekdays except Mondays; call (413) 548–9070.

For a truly wild ride, drive the aptly named Rattlesnake Gutter Road. To get there, follow the sign for Rattlesnake Gutter Road at the intersection of Dudleyville, North Leverett, and Church roads in North Leverett. Rattlesnake Gutter Road is a dirt road that climbs more than 1½ miles through a steep, densely wooded ravine. The road falls away sharply on either side, almost 100 feet down. Tangles of massive boulders and the huge, moss-covered trunks of fallen trees line the sides of the ravine. The temperature drops noticeably as you drive in the dark shadow of looming pines.

If you're a true off-the-beaten-path traveler, you'll seek out the abandoned charcoal kiln at the end of Rattlesnake Gutter Road. Charcoal was once a leading industry in town, and this kiln was used to make it. Just after you cross a little wooden bridge, turn left; then go ³⁄₁₀ mile, past a white warehouse and a brown house by a waterfall, and the charcoal kiln will be on your right. A round brick structure, the kiln looks like a giant beehive and is partly obscured by a field of goldenrod as high as your head. The kiln represented an advance over burning in pits in the woods to make charcoal. This kiln is one of only a few left in the state.

A great lunchtime stop off Route 202 is **Hamilton Orchards** (508–544–6867), a family orchard since the 1920s. There are all kinds of treats and activities here. You can pick your own apples, raspberries, and blueberries or watch the making of cider or maple syrup in season. A unique "doughnut robot" turns out cider doughnuts by the hour. In the barn and shop, the irresistible smells of warm apple pie and turnovers waft through the air. There are free apples for "kids of all ages" and a cafeteria serving apple dumplings, baked beans, hot dogs, and sundaes. The cafe is a cheery, hearty place, with a wood stove, red-and-white-checkered tablecloths, and a wall of windows looking out on a clean sweep of mountain and forest.

A restaurant that could not be more a part and piece of this area is the New Salem Store and Restaurant. The rustic dining room has a massive fireplace and old wooden booths and tables. The walls are a Quabbin art gallery: historic black-and-white photos of Swift River Valley families of 1910, beautiful color photos of wild birds and animals at the Quabbin, and aerial views of the scenic reservoir. The restaurant serves good homemade soups and breads, hot and cold sandwiches, and salads.

If a visit to the Quabbin Reservoir whetted your curiosity about the four towns flooded to create it, you can find out about them at the **Swift River Valley Historical Society** (508–544–6882), on Elm Street off Route 202. Three small buildings cluster together in a clearing: an early nineteenth-century white house, a church, and a red barn, all holding memorabilia from the four towns—Greenwich, Dana, Prescott, and Enfield. The church originally stood in North Prescott.

When I first visited in 1990, there were still people living who hailed from the Swift River Valley. An elderly man was able to show me his house on a diorama of the valley. The four towns were officially tolled out of existence in 1938. All 2,500 residents had to leave, and their homes were razed or relocated, businesses torn down, and cemeteries dug up. Nothing remained but old lanes and cellar holes. Such a sacrifice would be unheard of today. Among items saved by the historical society are a handwoven palmleaf hat made in Dana, hatmaking having been one of that town's principal industries; wedding gowns and lace handkerchiefs; and cameos and jewelry. The historical society buildings are open from 2:00 to 4:00 P.M. Wednesday and Sunday in July and August and only on Sundays from September to mid-October. Admission is $2.00.

In the nineteenth century, the town of Orange was a hive of industry. Like a miniature Lowell, it was laced with canals and brick factories and mills. Many mementos of this industrial past are kept at the **Orange Historical Society,** at 41 North Main Street. The museum is in a large Victorian home that rambles on forever. It was built in 1867 for Stephen French, cofounder of the first sewing machine company, the New Home Sewing Machine Company of Orange. A handful of New Home sewing machines, elaborately painted and housed in solid oak cabinets, are on exhibit.

By 1832, Orange had a wooden pail factory, a carding mill, a sawmill, a gristmill, a blacksmith, tanneries, a wheelwright and carriage shop, and a scythe factory. Orange is also where Minute Tapioca was invented, in 1894. The museum has a coffee grinder that was used in the first production of the tapioca and has pictures of the tapioca plant and vintage ads for the product. At the turn of the century, Orange made Grout Steam Cars, steam-powered cars that started with a match and that won prizes for hill climbing, speed, and endurance all over the world; on display at the museum is a 1904 Grout Steam Car.

Besides these hallmarks of industry, the museum holds large and varied collections of decorative arts and household memorabilia too numerous to list. They include china, pewter, and porcelain; dolls and dollhouses; antique iron cookware; hats, shoes, and jewelry; and military memorabilia. A barn houses antique fire vehicles, old plows and farm tools, and a 1915 World War I caisson. The museum is open from 2:00 to 4:00 P.M. Sundays and Wednesdays, mid-May through October; admission is $1.00. For information, call Irene Ballou, president of the historical society, at (508) 544–6286.

Springfield and Holyoke

Interstate 91 goes bombing right through the heart of these two busy cities. It's hard to find your way about here, but do take the trouble, because you'll be well rewarded. For travel information, contact the Greater Springfield Convention and Visitors Bureau, 34 Boland Way at Baystate West, Springfield 01103; (413) 787–1548.

The first stop is **Holyoke Heritage State Park** (413–534–1723), which colorfully chronicles the industrial history of Holyoke. In the nineteenth century, the city built a three-level canal system 4½ miles long to channel Connecticut River water to its mills, first to cotton mills and later to paper mills. Holyoke once had so many paper mills—some two dozen—that it was known as "Paper City" and made a great deal of the world's fine writing papers. You'll find lots of memorabilia of city residents, papermaking machinery, and a slide show about the industrial and social history of Holyoke. A railroad with vintage 1920s passenger cars occasionally runs through the park and through town (call for schedule). The landscaped grounds are also a fine spot for a picnic, overlooking a canal and several century-old red brick mill buildings. The park is located at 221 Appleton Street. Hours are noon to 4:30 P.M. Wednesday, Thursday, and Sunday (subject to change).

Adjacent to the park is the Volleyball Hall of Fame (413–536–0926), a tribute to the fact that volleyball was invented in Holyoke in 1895. Boldly painted, contemporary exhibits explain that volleyball was invented by a local YMCA physical education director who used a tennis net and the inside of a basketball and called his new game "mintonette." The museum, at 444 Dwight Street, is open from 10:00 A.M. to 5:00 P.M. Tuesday through Friday and from noon to 5:00 P.M. weekends.

Lots of factory outlets are situated in the heart of the city surrounding the heritage park, ranging from clothing and handcrafts to furniture and cookware. One of the more unusual outlets is Lady Bugs, Ltd., at 380 Dwight Street (413–533–8809), which sells dried flowers, wreaths, and country accessories. (For a list and map of outlets, write the Greater Springfield Convention and Visitors Bureau, noted above.)

A bright jewel not to be overlooked in Holyoke is **Wistari-ahurst Museum,** an elegant Victorian mansion that was the home of a wealthy silk manufacturer. Lavishly decorated with stained glass, parquet floors, coffered ceilings, and a marble lobby, the home also holds many period furnishings and paintings. A Renaissance-style music hall is a frequent venue for concerts, as this fine mansion serves as a cultural center for the city.

Also on the grounds are landscaped gardens and a carriage house containing North American Indian and natural history exhibits. Wistariahurst is at 238 Cabot Street in Holyoke; call (413) 534–2216. Admission is $2.00. Hours are from 1:00 to 5:00 P.M. Wednesdays and from noon to 5:00 P.M. weekends.

A Holyoke fixture since 1947, the Yankee Pedlar Inn, at 1866 Northampton Street (413–532–9494), serves such hearty, traditional fare as a New England boiled dinner, prime rib, and chicken potpie, as well as seafood.

Downtown Springfield boasts a cultural centerpiece in four important museums, all handily arranged in a quadrangle off State Street and Chestnut Avenue, called the **Springfield Museum Quadrangle.** There is not one but two major art museums. The George Walter Vincent Smith Art Museum houses the collection of the Victorian gentleman it's named after, who collected what he liked: Japanese arms, Chinese cloisonné, and Oriental jades, textiles, and ceramics. The Museum of Fine Arts holds twenty centuries of art, including impressionist, expressionist, and early European paintings, and works by Helen Frankenthaler and Georgia O'Keeffe. A more fun place for children is the Science Museum, which invites children to touch many exhibits and which also has a planetarium. At the Connecticut Valley Historical Museum, you can see many fine decorative artworks made by Connecticut River Valley residents, including pewter, silver, furniture, and the work of itinerant portrait painters. Early valley life is illustrated by a colonial kitchen, a Federal dining room, and two nineteenth-century tavern rooms brought here. The museums are open from noon to 5:00 P.M. daily except Monday. For information, call the Springfield Library and Museums Association at (413) 739–3871.

In the late nineteenth century, Springfield had so many fine Victorian homes set on tree-lined streets that it earned the nickname "City of Homes." Hundreds of these houses still stand, and two areas are now historic districts. The **McKnight District** has almost 900 Victorian houses built between 1870 and 1900. Huge, rambling affairs, they have wide porches and, often, carriage houses and stables. The McKnight District centers on Worthington Street; call (413) 736–8583 for information. Another collection of houses can be seen on **Mattoon Street,** 1 block north of Museum Quadrangle. These fine old Victorian row houses of the 1870s, reminiscent of those in Boston's Back Bay, represent Springfield's only street lined with brick row houses. The houses have been nicely complemented by gaslight-style streetlights and tree-shaded brick walks. This neighborhood sponsors an antiques show in early June and a street arts festival in early September.

The **Student Prince and Fort Restaurant,** at 8 Fort Street (413–734–7475), has been a much-loved local institution since 1935. Its Old World German feeling is created by stained-glass windows, wood-paneled booths, and a priceless collection of some 1,500 antique beer steins lining the shelves of its dining room walls. Some steins are one of a kind; one once belonged to a Russian czar. The stained-glass windows show classic scenes of Springfield and Germany.

The German and American menu lists such specialties as oxtail soup, hasenpfeffer, jaeger schnitzel, and sauerbraten. You'll find all kinds of German beers on draft, as well as many wines and European liqueurs. To add to the fun, the restaurant throws festivals several times a year. In February, a Game Fest serves pheasant, buffalo, venison, and bear. A May Wine Fest and an Oktoberfest are also popular. And at Christmastime, the Fort puts up decorations and brings in carolers.

Even if you're not a military buff, you'll find the **Springfield Armory National Historic Site** an interesting place. George Washington chose Springfield as the site for a national arsenal in 1794. The armory and weapons made there played a major role in every American war thereafter. On and around the armory green stand a number of original buildings, including the Main Arsenal, the Commanding Officer's Quarters, and the Master Armorer's House.

The weapons housed in the Main Arsenal form the world's largest collection of small arms. Here you can see the Springfield rifle used in World War I and the famous M–1 rifle used by millions of servicemen in World War II. The armory is located at One Armory Square and is open daily from 9:00 A.M. to 5:00 P.M. Call (413) 734–8551.

Springfield is also the birthplace of the motorcyle, invented in 1901, when bicycle-racing champion George Hendee teamed up with C. Oscar Hedstrom to open the Indian Motocyle Manufacturing Company (they dropped the "r" as an advertising ploy). The famous Indian Motocyle the company produced was known worldwide for quality and beauty. In World War I, more than half the army motorcycles in use were Indians. In its heyday, the company also made airplane engines, bicycles, and outboard motors. You can see a large collection of Indian Motocyles, toy motorcycles, and memorabilia at the Indian Motocycle Museum, at 33 Hendee Street (413–737–2624). An annual Indian Day rally attracts proud Indian owners from all over the country. The museum is open from 10:00 A.M. to 5:00 P.M. daily; admission is $3.00 for adults and $1.00 for children.

Although not so well known as Old Sturbridge Village, **Stor-**

rowton Village Museum was established much earlier. A collection of nine eighteenth- and nineteenth-century buildings were brought here in the 1920s from all over New England and were arranged like the heart of an old New England village. Besides a meetinghouse and church, there are a blacksmith, tavern, and school. Because of its small size, this attraction offers a much more intimate experience than Old Sturbridge Village. Storrowton Village is on the grounds of the Eastern States Exposition, off Memorial Avenue in West Springfield; call (413) 787–0136. Admission is $3.00 for adults and $2.00 for children. Tours are given from 11:00 A.M. to 3:00 P.M. daily, except Sunday, from mid-June through October.

Author Thornton Burgess, who wrote tales of Peter Rabbit and *Old Mother West Wind,* once lived in Hampden. His former home can be toured and is now part of Laughing Brook Education Center and Wildlife Sanctuary. Several miles of hiking trails take you through woodlands and fields, past streams and a pond. An intriguing addition made in 1990 is the Northeast Habitats Exhibit, an arrangement of boardwalks and observation towers that let you see animals in their habitats, just as sophisticated zoos have taken to doing. Among the animals here are white-tailed deer, bobcats, coyote, turkey vultures, and barred owls. The sanctuary, located at 789 Main Street in Hampden, is open from 10:00 A.M. to 5:00 P.M. Tuesday through Sunday. Admission is $3.00 for adults and $1.50 for children. Call (413) 566–8034.

Off the Beaten Path in the Berkshires

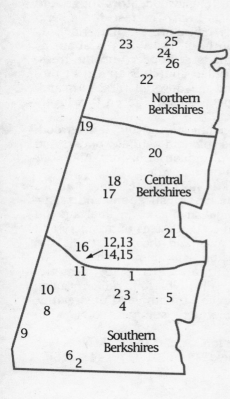

1. Gingerbread House
2. Bidwell House
3. Joyous Spring Pottery
4. Rawson Brook Farm
5. Otis Poultry Farm
6. Bartholomew's Cobble
7. Colonel John Ashley House
8. Gaslight Store
9. Bash Bish Falls
10. Albert Schweitzer Center
11. Monument Mountain Reservation
12. Ice Glen
13. Children's Chimes
14. Marian Center
15. Naumkeag
16. Berkshire Garden Center
17. Pleasant Valley Wildlife Sanctuary
18. Arrowhead
19. Hancock Shaker Village
20. Crane Paper Museum
21. Becket General Store
22. Mount Greylock
23. Sterling and Francine Clark Art Institute
24. Western Gateway Heritage State Park
25. Natural Bridge
26. Squeeze Beverages

The Berkshires

If manicured lawns and black tie are not your style, don't despair. All that centers in the Tanglewood, Stockbridge, and Lenox area, where most tourists head. The rest of the Berkshires, north and south, seems to be a great deal overlooked.

The countryside of the southern Berkshires is about as bucolic as it gets. Country roads disappear into the trees; small villages with white-steepled churches appear at rare intervals among the fields and meadows of rural farmland. Not a few artists and craftspeople have chosen this lovely hinterland for their home.

Almost no one thinks of heading north from Tanglewood. But if you do, you'll find some splendid natural wonders and old mill towns with a patina of industrial history. And your travels there will be wonderfully uncrowded.

Still, the central Berkshires is no place to sneeze at. It's here that world-famous cultural sophistications and scenic beauty come together in a unique amalgam, an amalgam you won't find anywhere else in the state. Acres of greenery and stately mountains embrace dance and theater festivals and the summer home of the Boston Symphony Orchestra. The inspiring beauty of the mountains attracted Nathaniel Hawthorne, Herman Melville, Edith Wharton, William Cullen Bryant, and Henry James. They in turn attracted the wealthy, who found it chic to build enormous summer "cottages" in the Gilded Era.

For complete travel information, contact the Berkshires Visitors Bureau, Box IFP 90, Pittsfield MA 01201; (413) 443–9186.

Southern Berkshires

Winding country roads make it impossible not to double back on your tracks around here, but you won't mind in this most scenic New England of yesteryear, composed of farms, ponds, meadows of Queen Anne's lace, and pastures full of cows. Going south on Route 102 from Lee, take the narrow Tyringham-Monterey Road. Eventually you'll come to a little

Gingerbread House

thatched cottage, densely shadowed by a grove of trees, that looks for all the world exactly like the fairy-tale house of Hansel and Gretel. Grottoes of stone reach up the walls to the rolling curves of its roof. The **Gingerbread House** (officially, the Tyringham Art Galleries) belonged to the late sculptor Sir Henry Kitson, an unusual person who used it as his studio.

Kitson sculpted the *Minute Man* at Lexington and also the *Puritan Maid* at Plymouth. Here at his studio, a stone walk with abstract sculptures leads to wild gardens and a little pond where Sir Henry kept goldfish—he fed them oatmeal and called them by name. While the outside is intriguing enough, the gallery exhibits paintings, sculptures, and ceramics of artists from local and regional to national stature. The galleries have a mystical, medieval feeling, with Gothic-arched stone doorways, stained-glass windows, a stone floor, and a beamed cathedral ceiling. Visit the gallery from 10:00 A.M. to 5:00 P.M. daily, Memorial Day to Labor Day (weekends only until October 17). Admission is 50 cents. Call (413) 243–3260.

A little farther south on the Tyringham-Monterey Road you come to a dirt road on the left called Art School Road. It leads to the historic **Bidwell House,** high on a hill in the forest. In a region not overflowing with historic houses, this one is a real jewel.

The Reverend Adonijah Bidwell built the house around 1750, soon after he came to Monterey to set up a church. The luxury of this white Georgian saltbox house is illuminating to those of us expecting ascetic surroundings. Son of a wealthy merchant, Reverend Bidwell furnished his house with nothing but the best: elegantly carved paneling, beautiful colors of cranberry and blue, and two beehive ovens. Among the fine goods are imported gold and embroidered fabrics, patterned carpets, canopied four-posters, redware, pewter, English delft china, and six punch bowls. Listed on the National Register of Historic Places, the house was opened to the public in 1990. Hours are 11:00 A.M. to 4:00 P.M. Tuesday through Sunday and holidays, May 26 through October 14. Admission is $4.00 for adults, $3.00 for seniors and students, and $2.00 for children. Call (413) 528–6988 for information.

Also on Art School Road you'll find **Joyous Spring Pottery,** a unique, one-man gallery. Many pairs of visitors' shoes sit on the deck outside the glass doors, removed in honor of the Japanese-style salon. Owner Michael Marcus works in a most unusual vein, an ancient Japanese technique called *yaki-shime,* which he studied in Japan; only a handful of craftspeople in this country know it. Rather than using glazes, this method lets molten ash from a wood-fired kiln create random patterns in tans, browns, pale yellows, and siennas. Marcus built his own Japanese-style, multichambered climbing kiln to get these results. His showroom is filled with many curved and rounded pieces based on such traditional forms as sake bottles, sushi plates, and tea ceremony pieces. Although this pottery is expensive, it's also exquisite and very beautiful. The gallery is open from 10:00 A.M. to 5:00 P.M. daily; call (413) 528–4115.

The Tyringham-Monterey Road, naturally enough, brings you into tiny Monterey, on Route 23, Monterey's main street. The center of town is the Monterey General Store, right next door to the post office. The store's white-columned porch shelters two wooden benches and a sign listing the goods of 1780, when the store was established: spices, molasses, beeswax, hops, tinware, burlap, awls, castor oil, seeds, and rock candy, among others. Inside is more modern merchandise, as well as a small coffee shop that is a popular gathering place for socializing and gossip. Across the street is a small antiques store.

One of the best goat cheeses is produced right in Monterey: Monterey Chèvre, made by a young couple at **Rawson Brook Farm** (413–528–2138). Wayne Dunlop and Susan Sellew like living off the land in a simple way and raising their young daughter on a farm. They keep a herd of French and American Alpine goats, with their names printed on green collar tags—Vanilla, Azaline, Anisette, and Mocha, for example. You are welcome to visit the farm and see the pretty goats out in the fields. You can watch them being milked in the "milk parlor" from April 1 through November 1, around 4:30 P.M. Five kinds of chèvre are sold from a tall, steel refrigerator in the milking parlor: plain chèvre, chèvre with chives and garlic, chèvre with no salt, chèvre with thyme and olive oil, and peppered logs of chèvre.

To reach Rawson Brook Farm, follow the signs just past the general store, taking the first right off Route 23 heading east. Because Wayne and Susan live there, you can visit the farm almost anytime, but they ask that you not be unreasonable about this.

There's another farm just east of Monterey on Route 8 in Otis. North of Otis, the road passes by some little red chicken coops on the right, each bearing a single word painted in big white letters. The signs are really designed to be read as you're heading south, and so if you can't quite make them out, turn around and go the other way. If you slow down, you can read what they say: EGG/EATERS/MAKE/BETTER/LOVERS, and FARM/FRESH/EGGS/LAID/HERE. The coops signal the **Otis Poultry Farm,** where a sign proudly announces HOME OF FAMOUS CHICKEN GICKEM FERTILIZER—YOUR GARDEN'S BEST FRIEND. Is that stuff really good for the garden? "Damn tootin'," says a clerk. The farm's store holds not only fresh chickens, eggs, and chicken pies but unexpected racks of wooden model train kits, shearling-lined moccasins, fringed leather jackets, and woven baskets.

Weekday mornings, you can tour the farm, see eggs candled, and get an earful of the ruckus that 24,000 chickens kick up. Call (413) 269–4438 for information.

Tiny Mill River takes its name from the many paper mills there in the mid-1800s. There are the requisite general store and town hall, both charming. But more interesting is a wonderful gallery, the Gallery at Mill River (413–229–2018), situated in an attractive restored barn. Besides his own paintings and cityscape collages, owner Lewis Barrett Lehrman shows Berkshire artists' work and that of artists from as far afield as the Soviet Union. He always puts out lemonade and cookies for visitors. The gallery is open daily from 11:00 A.M. to 5:00 P.M. June 30 to Labor Day and only on weekends to October 21.

If you're in need of some quiet respite, you'll find it not far from the gallery. About 1 mile south of the bridge into Mill River, on the Clayton-Mill River Road, there's a sign saying UMPACHENE FALLS. A dirt road leads to a rushing river by a small park. The falls lie a short walk away under a mantle of pines. Large boulders offer nice vantage points to gaze at the falls and listen to the play of water falling from terrace to terrace over its ½-mile course. In the pool below, small children swim in hot weather.

A short detour east of Mill River is a shopping bonanza, the Buggy Whip Factory (413–229–8280) in Southfield—old wooden buildings that once actually housed an eighteenth-century buggy whip factory. Now they hold shops, factory outlets, dozens of antiques dealers, crafts retailers, and a cafe. The complex is located on Route 272, across from the fire department.

The southwest corner of the southern Berkshires embraces two lovely spots, **Bartholomew's Cobble** and the historic **Colonel John Ashley House,** adjoining properties of the Trustees of Reservations (413–229–8600).

The word *cobble* means rocky-topped hill, and it's a remarkable natural phenomenon. Bartholomew's Cobble is only the second National Natural Landmark to be so designated in Massachusetts (the first is Gay Head Cliffs on Martha's Vineyard). The two marble outcroppings here formed 500 million years ago from recrystallized limestone. The limy soil nurtured many unusual ferns and other rock-dwelling plants, including maidenhair spleenwort, columbine, and hairbells. Besides some 53 kinds of ferns, there are almost 500 species of wildflowers and 100 species of trees.

This sylvan setting is a wonderful place to walk, with about 6 miles of trails. The very short Eaton Trail up the cobble can be climbed in a few minutes, rewarding the climber with a peaceful view of the Housatonic River Valley and grazing cows on green meadows. Take time to visit the rustic little museum holding animal and plant specimens, along with Indian relics.

Bartholomew's Cobble is open from 9:00 A.M. to 5:00 P.M. daily from mid-April to mid-October; the museum closes Mondays and Tuesdays. Admission is $3.00 for adults and $1.00 for children.

In colonial days, Bartholomew's Cobble was owned by Colonel John Ashley, a wealthy merchant and lawyer and the leading citizen of Sheffield. His two-story wood-frame house, built in 1735, is the oldest in Berkshire County.

As you step into the cool, dim interior of the Colonel John Ashley House, the years fall away to that much more primitive time. Still, Colonel Ashley imported craftsmen from far and wide to create intricately carved paneling and moldings, boxed ceiling beams, and, in his study, an exquisite, sunburst-topped cupboard. There's a fine collection of redware and Benningtonware in the buttery.

In his study, Colonel Ashley and a committee drafted the Sheffield Declaration of 1773, which prefigured the Declaration of Independence. It also inspired an Ashley family slave named Mum Bett to seek her freedom. With Colonel Ashley's help, she became the first freed slave in Massachusetts. The Ashley House adjoins Bartholomew's Cobble, off Route 7A in Ashley Falls, well marked by signs. It's open from 1:00 to 5:00 P.M. Wednesday through Sunday and holidays, May 25 to October 14. Tickets cost $3.50 for adults and $1.00 for children.

Sheffield is home to the oldest covered bridge in Massachusetts, the Sheffield Covered Bridge, built in 1835. To get to the bridge, head north on Route 7 and look for the sign on the left, just opposite the American Legion Post. Another historic note here is that the last battle of Shays' Rebellion was fought in Sheffield. In this altercation, angry revolutionary war veterans struck back at a government that seized their debt-ridden property and would not accept the same money it had paid to them as tax payments.

Strung out along narrow and winding Route 23, South Egremont is like a little village lost in time. The whole downtown, including a pretty white church and town hall, is a National Historic District.

The nineteenth century lives on at the **Gaslight Store** (413–528–0870), where you can still buy an egg cream and purchase penny candy for a penny. An egg cream has neither egg nor cream in it but tastes delicious all the same. Like an ice-cream soda without ice cream, it's made with syrup, seltzer, and milk. The owner makes no profit on his penny candy but prices it that way anyway, to keep tradition alive.

The store has been there for 150 years and still has the original marble ice-cream counter. On shelves stand antique boxes of Rinso and Ivory Snow, Royal baking powder, and Lydia Pinkham tablets, as well as old-fashioned glassware. Ice-cream-parlor chairs with heart-shaped backs and red-and-white-checkered tablecloths add to the vintage feeling. An antique cash register beautifully repousséed in bronze sits ready to ring up purchases.

Several doors away, Mom's Country Cafe (413–528–2414) offers down-home cheer exuded by friendly waitresses, homemade food, gingham curtains, and tables made out of old sewing machines. Breakfast is served all day. A more formal eatery in town is the Old Mill (413–528–1421), a restored 1797 gristmill and blacksmith's shop also on Route 23.

Tucked into the very southwest corner of the state, bordering on New York, is the wildest countryside you'll encounter in the southern Berkshires. A narrow rutted road with dizzying switchbacks dips and swoops up and down Mount Washington, winding through towering and dark forest. Long before you get to the spectacular 80-foot waterfall that barrels down the mountainside—**Bash Bish Falls**—you'll swear you're lost in the wilderness.

Indian legend has it that a beautiful Indian maiden, White Swan, hurled herself into the falls to her death. Two paths lead down to the falls. One is so unbelievably steep that it looks as though only world-champion rock climbers should attempt it; the other, a wide gravel path, descends to a point just above the falls. From Route 23, take Route 41 south and

then take an immediate right onto Mount Washington Road.
Follow signs first for Mount Washington State Forest and
then for Bash Bish Falls. Call (413) 528–0330 for information.

For a restful and serene stay, try Hidden Acres Bed & Breakfast, deep in the woods in North Egremont. A deer may flash
across the road at dusk, and wild turkeys and occasional red
foxes come about in the mornings, as do lots of birds. Owners Danny and Lorraine Moore built the house themselves,
using 150-year-old post-and-beam contruction. Guest rooms
are ample and are decorated in pastel colors and lace curtains (doubles, $55–$75). Full breakfasts include blueberry
pancakes or French toast. Call (413) 528–1028, or write the
owners at RD 4, Box 150, Great Barrington 01230.

Busy Great Barrington brims with restaurants, some of the
nicest of them on Railroad Street, just off Route 7 downtown,
a little enclave that also mixes in several intriguing boutiques. Among the eateries here are La Tomate (413–
528–3003), an upbeat little bistro that feels very French and
serves excellent French food, and Martin's (413–528–5455),
offering all-day breakfast and blackboard specials, homemade muffins and soups, and homemade desserts. Around
the corner from Railroad Street, at 10 Castle Street, is the
Castle Street Cafe (413–528–5244), a citified cafe whose
sophisticated chef makes such ambitious dishes as coho
salmon stuffed with mushroom mousse, as well as other
American and Continental fare.

As you're driving south on Route 7 in the center of town,
don't miss a peek left through the gates at Searles Castle,
built by railroad magnate Mark Hopkins's widow. Great Barrington also hosts a unique music festival in July, the Aston
Magna Festival. This is America's oldest and premier festival
of seventeenth- and eighteenth-century music played on
original baroque-period instruments. For information, call
(413) 528–3595, or write Aston Magna Festival, P.O. Box 1035,
Great Barrington 01230.

For a contemplative cap to your Great Barrington visit, stop
in at the **Albert Schweitzer Center** (413–528–3124),
founded by a documentary filmmaker friend of Schweitzer's.
A 150-year-old red farmhouse houses a library, auditorium,
and memorabilia, including ivory tusks decoratively carved
by grateful leper patients. A film explains Schweitzer's early

life as a philosopher and musician of some means and his lifelong philosophy of a "reverence for life." It also shows Schweitzer in his signature black bow tie, shaggy white mustache, and pith helmet, surrounded by his patients and beloved animals, including a pelican called Parsifal who followed him everywhere. Schweitzer served his patients at the hospital he built in Lambarene, Gabon, until his death in 1965 at the age of ninety.

There's a wildlife sanctuary on the grounds too, a peaceful little wooded clearing by a brook. The center is open from 10:00 A.M. to 4:00 P.M. Tuesday through Sunday and from noon to 4:00 P.M. Sunday, April 16 to October 31, and from 11:00 A.M. to 4:00 P.M., November 1 to April 15. It's located on Hurlburt Road, marked by signs from Taconic Road off Route 23 in downtown Great Barrington, just past the town hall.

Central Berkshires

On your way to Stockbridge, you'll see **Monument Mountain Reservation** on Route 7, about 2½ miles south of town. This mountain was the scene of what has been called the world's most famous literary picnic. Herman Melville, Nathaniel Hawthorne, and Oliver Wendell Holmes climbed it on an August day in 1850. Dressed in their frock coats, they admired the view, lunched among the rocks, and toasted William Cullen Bryant. This craggy mountain rises some 1,700 feet to wonderful scenic views. At the entrance are picnic tables shaded by pines.

In Stockbridge, hordes of people clump about the porch of the Red Lion Inn, congregate on Main Street around the shops, and visit the Norman Rockwell Museum to see the local streets painted into fame by this popular artist. But there are some quieter spots here as well.

One, the **Ice Glen**, is a great place for a walk on a hot day. The Ice Glen was carved out by a glacier, leaving massive boulders where the sun never reaches. It has been said that you can find ice crystals there even in summer, although more likely the rocks are just moist. When you stand in front of these moss-covered rocks, it's as cool as opening a refrigerator door. This mystical place used to be the site of Halloween bonfires and torchlight parades.

To reach the Ice Glen, turn onto Park Road off Route 7 just south of downtown Stockbridge. Park at the end of the turnaround. Over the wooden footbridge, the right branch of the trail leads up to the Ice Glen, about a 15- to 20-minute walk.

Right on Main Street are two attractions that most people don't pay any attention to. One is a tall stone tower, sort of Gothic-looking. It's the **Children's Chimes,** a carillon given to the town in 1878 by David Dudley Field, Jr., in honor of his grandchildren. Field left money for the chimes to be played, by hand, from apple blossom time until frost.

The other site, located across the street in the town cemetery, is one of the country's most unusual family plots, "the Sedgwick Pie." It's shaped like a pie, with dozens of headstones and monuments in varying shapes and sizes placed in concentric rings, all facing toward the center. Legend has it that this design was intended to make sure the Sedgwicks saw only Sedgwicks when they woke up on Judgment Day, but that notion has been categorically denied by more than one Sedgwick. Generations of Sedgwicks have been buried in the pie, eschewing fancy coffins and wearing their pajamas. To see the pie, walk through the cemetery toward the right back corner.

Just north of Main Street are yet two more inviting places. One of the most beautiful spots in town is the **Marian Center** monastery on Eden Hill, founded by an order that originated in Poland. A long drive leads up to grassy lawns surrounding the abbey and an exquisite stone chapel. The grounds are an inspiring place for a walk or picnic, and no one should miss seeing the chapel. Inside it are marvelous stained-glass windows of saints; frescoes; marble altars; gospel scenes; and a magnificent Rose Window. The craftsmanship of all these creations rivals that of the great cathedrals of Europe, and indeed the work was led by an Italian master stonecutter.

The second inviting spot stands across from the Marian Center—**Naumkeag,** a quirky, turrety-looking mansion designed in 1885 by Stanford White for lawyer and diplomat Joseph Choate, who served as ambassador to England. The twenty-six-room house is full of offbeat personality, as White intended it to be. Turrets and bay windows are asymmetrical and appear at odd places.

Inside and out, this Norman-style, shingled-and-gabled mansion radiates the extravagance of the Gilded Age. The spacious rooms have high ceilings and mahogany trim. A Waterford crystal chandelier and silk-damask-patterned walls highlight the drawing room. Rare Chinese porcelains collected by Choate's daughter, Mabel, are on view, as are drawings and paintings by Choate's wife, who was an artist. An elegant, red-carpeted staircase with rope-turned balusters leads up to the seven bedrooms. President McKinley stayed in the master guest bedroom when he visited the Choates.

On the veranda, you can admire the expansive views of the azure Berkshire Hills dropping off below you. The gardens are among the loveliest in America, graced with a topiary promenade, Venetian-style posts, a Chinese pagoda, and a linden walk archway. Naumkeag is located on Prospect Hill Road. The house and gardens are open daily except Monday from late May through Labor Day and weekends and holidays through Columbus Day. Hours are 10:00 A.M. to 4:15 P.M. Admission is $5.00 for the house and gardens, $4.00 for the house only, and $3.00 for the gardens only. Call (413) 298–3239.

Before you leave Stockbridge, stop in at the **Berkshire Garden Center,** 2 miles west on Route 102. At the visitor center, you can get a self-guiding map to the gardens and greenhouses. Among the prettiest displays are a massive stand of daylilies in glowing pinks, yellows, and oranges; a primrose walk; a rose garden; and a small pond thickly growing with pond lilies and cattails. Also here are a diminutive herb garden, wildflowers, and many trees and shrubs. The gardens are a nice place to spend an afternoon or have a picnic. The center and gardens are open mid-May to mid-October from 10:00 A.M. to 5:00 P.M. Admission is $4.00 for adults and $1.00 for children. (Greenhouses stay open year-round and admission is free in winter.) Call (413) 298–3926.

If you keep going west on Route 102, you'll end up on the main street of West Stockbridge, a small village that is always less crowded than Stockbridge and is much more quaint. West Stockbridge still has its library and town clerk's office in a white house dating to 1774. A cluster of crafts shops, art galleries, antiques stores, clothing boutiques, and restaurants lines both sides of the street, going back several blocks. There's a little outdoor cafe at Beethoven's, which also sells baked goods, gifts, and jewelry. For a quick bite, stop into the Depot Cafe in the railroad station.

Alternatively, hop back on the Massachusetts Turnpike and go one exit down to Lee, to Joe's Diner, at 63 Center Street (413–243–9756), just off exit 2. This unpretentious place was the setting for Norman Rockwell's famous painting *The Runaway,* depicting a little boy with his sack of belongings nervously eyeing a cop sitting on a diner stool. Your regular diner fare is available here twenty-four hours a day, as is a 25-cent cup of coffee.

Another inexpensive Lee eatery is Athena's Pizza, at 20 Housatonic Street (413–243–1215), where besides Greek spinach pie, pizzas, grinders, and such homemade soups as beef vegetable and chicken rice, you'll get the best breakfast around, according to the jammed parking lot every morning. Nothing fancy—just eggs, toast, home fries, and omelets—but all well cooked and served in a convivial atmosphere.

Lovely Lenox was once a nucleus of millionaires' mansions, helping to win the Berkshires its nickname of "the Inland Newport." When the noted actress Fanny Kemble suggested a benefit for the village poor, she was told, "But we have no poor." Novelist Edith Wharton had her home at The Mount, now open to the public and the setting for Shakespeare & Company productions of Shakespeare plays.

Today Lenox is a verdant place, still well used to the well heeled. Fine shops and restaurants stand ready to serve them. Every summer, thousands throng the lawns of Tanglewood just outside Lenox to hear the Boston Symphony Orchestra.

Right across the street from the black iron gates of Tanglewood is a small red house on Hawthorne Street often overlooked by concertgoers, the Hawthorne Cottage. Nathaniel Hawthorne once lived here, though the original structure burned down. He was inspired to write *The House of the Seven Gables* here, and he befriended Herman Melville during his stay. Although Tanglewood musicians use the house as practice studios, it's open to the public for its displays of Hawthorne memorabilia. Admission is free.

Hawthorne Street intersects with Lake Road, which winds along the Stockbridge Bowl. This large lake, ringed with forests and mountains, is so blue and beautiful that it will remind you of a Swiss lake.

The most entertaining thing about the **Pleasant Valley Wildlife Sanctuary** has to be the beaver dams and lodges you can see in two ponds. Besides nature's oldest engineers, the 7 miles of trails show off uplands and meadows, a hemlock gorge, a hummingbird garden, and a limestone cobble. There are also a natural history museum and lots of programs, including bird and wildflower walks. The sanctuary is located at 472 West Mountain Road. To get there, follow Routes 7 and 20 north till you see the blue-and-white Audubon sign on the left, opposite the All Season Motor Inn; then turn left onto West Dugway Road and follow signs to West Mountain Road. Pleasant Valley is open from dawn to dusk Tuesday through Sunday. Admission is $3.00 for adults and $2.00 for children. Museum hours are from 10:00 A.M. to 4:00 P.M. weekends, mid-May through mid-June and September through October, and daily from June through August. Call (413) 637–0320.

Hawthorne's new friend Melville lived not far north from him in a quiet country home outside Pittsfield called **Arrowhead.** From his piazza, Melville had a wide-open view of Mount Greylock, which he thought resembled a great white whale; the view inspired him to write most of *Moby Dick* here between 1850 and 1851. In the Chimney Room, parts of the chimney are inscribed with words from Melville's short story "I and My Chimney." Upstairs, you can see his study, with some of his quill pens and his spectacles still on the table.

Behind this eighteenth-century yellow farmhouse stand stately willow and apple trees, along with a red barn, a place where Melville was fond of chatting with Hawthorne. Somewhere outside, a resident orange tiger cat may show himself. His name? Call him Ishmael.

Arrowhead is at 780 Holmes Road off Route 7 just south of Pittsfield, clearly marked by signs. Hours are from 10:00 A.M. to 4:30 P.M. Monday through Saturday and from 11:00 A.M. to 3:30 P.M. Sunday, Memorial Day weekend to October 31. (The house is closed Tuesdays and Wednesdays after Labor Day.) Admission is $3.50 for adults, $3.00 for senior citizens, and $2.00 for children. Call (413) 442–1793.

The **Hancock Shaker Village,** 5 miles west of Pittsfield, is

Round Stone Barn, Hancock Shaker Village

a major tourist attraction and often crowded. Still, this is the best place to learn about the unique chapter in New England history written by the Shakers. This unusual sect, founded in 1774, earned the derisive name of Shakers because of their active style of singing and dancing at worship.

The Shaker community at Hancock reached its height in the 1840s, with about 250 members. Women served alongside men as eldresses and deacons, and everyone worked together at dairying, furnituremaking, handweaving, and basketry. They became famous for the high quality of their products, particularly the furniture and oval-shaped wooden boxes.

Twenty of their original brick and wooden buildings stand scattered about the green landscape. A stroll among them on a sparkling sunny day is pleasant and is in distinct contrast to the severity of the Shakers' lives. In the Brick Dwelling, where the brethren and sisters lived, rising was at 4:30 A.M.

but breakfast was not until 7:00. The sexes sat separately at plain wooden tables and ate in silence.

Drawing people like a talisman, the Round Stone Barn is a thing of beauty, topped with a white cupola, and yet is eminently practical: It allowed one man standing alone in it to milk fifty-four cows. Other buildings show the work of everyday life: the washhouse, the tannery, the icehouse, and the poultry house.

Most days, there's a program: Shaker hymn music, baking or boxmaking demonstrations, or spinning and weaving. Occasionally, Shaker-style candlelight dinners are served.

Hancock Shaker Village is open daily from April through November. Hours are from 9:30 A.M. to 5:00 P.M. Memorial Day weekend to October 31 and from 10:00 A.M. to 3:00 P.M. during April, May, and November. Admission is $8.50 for adults and $4.00 for children. Call (413) 443–0188.

Outside the handsome brick downtown of Pittsfield are the large mills of Crane & Co., papermakers for almost 200 years. Just past the mills, 5 miles east of Pittsfield off Route 9, there's a sign for the **Crane Paper Museum** in Dalton.

Crane is the only company that makes paper for the U.S. government to print money on, a contract it has held since 1879. Paul Revere was the company's first banknote engraver. The seventh generation of Cranes is at work in the mills. The company has made nothing but fine rag papers ever since the first mill was built, in 1801. Because of its consistently high quality, Crane paper was traditionally used in the nineteenth century for official documents, deeds, titles, and financial instruments and came to be known as bond paper. Until 1845, the paper was entirely made by hand, a single sheet at a time.

The museum is in an ivy-covered stone building with stairstep gables, a former rag room. On view are historic currency samples, exhibits on papermaking, and many samples of letterheads and invitations. It's open from 2:00 to 5:00 P.M. Monday through Friday. Call (413) 684–2600.

There's no good way to get to Becket. And that's how townspeople like it. (You can get there by taking Route 8 south from Dalton.) The town of Becket is about as hinterland as it gets in the central Berkshires. Bypassed entirely by the Massachusetts Turnpike, Becket has kept itself in its own little time warp, remaining rural and undeveloped. Its population numbers only 1,600. The few buildings that constitute downtown Becket huddle together for encouragement along a short stretch of Route 8. As an intriguing counterpoint, one of the most prestigious dance festivals in the world is held here—Jacob's Pillow.

If you're a connoisseur of general stores, you'll find the **Becket General Store** the most idiosyncratically genuine of the many to be found in the central and southern Berkshires. Local men and women line up at the small counter in the morning in a steady and constant stream. Some sit down to sip coffee and munch doughnuts; others buy newspapers. The shelves hem together so narrowly that two people cannot pass each other without do-si-do-ing down the aisles. Cramming the shelves is a hodgepodge of merchandise that would do a nineteenth-century general store proud: fishing lures next to birthday candles; such toys as Slinkys, crayons, and Wiffle balls; shampoo and cough syrup; kitchen gadgets; and, in a nod to modernity, rental videos. Cardboard boxes full of potatoes, peaches, tomatoes, and bananas slump on the floor.

Just up the hill past the general store on High Street is a real down-home bed-and-breakfast inn, the 1820 Long House. A rambling white farmhouse built around 1820, the inn has a wraparound porch that catches the afternoon sun, showing off pretty pink and white impatiens and white wicker. Owners Joan and Roy Simmons are as unpretentious as their rooms: the sheets may not match the quilt, but you'll always feel welcome. The bed-and-breakfast is convenient for Appalachian Trail hikers. (Doubles cost $35–$60, with private and shared baths; full breakfast is included.) Call (413) 623–8360, or write the owners at High Street, Becket 01223.

From Becket, you can take the Pittsfield Road right off Route 8, which eventually brings you back out to Routes 7 and 20.

Northern Berkshires

Heading north on Route 7, you'll pass Pontoosuc Lake on the left. This is a nice place to sailboard or canoe, and there are rental outlets along the shore. For a scenic detour, take Peck's

Road, a left turn that loops almost completely around the lake.

Mighty **Mount Greylock,** at 3,491 feet, is the state's highest peak. From its summit, you can see five states and up to 100 miles. The 10,000-acre reservation is popular for camping, for hiking and cross-country skiing along its 45 miles of trails, or for just plain seeking tranquillity from its rugged heights. A highlight of a visit here is the War Veterans Memorial Tower, built in 1932 at the summit and originally designed as a lighthouse.

You can drive up the south side of the mountain from Lanesboro, and down the north side in North Adams. From Route 7 north of Lanesboro, you'll see the entrance road. A short distance in, a visitor center holds displays on natural history. The season opens at Mount Greylock when "mountain spring" arrives, usually sometime in mid-May, and closes in October. Call (413) 499–4262 for information. Those who love informality will welcome a stay at Bascom Lodge at the summit, a rustic stone-and-wood building constructed by the Civilian Conservation Corps in the 1930s. Bascom Lodge is run by the Appalachian Mountain Club, which offers private and dormitory-style rooms, plus family-style breakfast and dinner. For information, write AMC–Bascom Lodge, P.O. Box 686, Lanesboro 01237, or call (413) 743–1591.

Route 7 joins the Mohawk Trail (Route 2) near the Massachusetts-Vermont border, formerly a Mohawk Indian invasion route and now a scenic fall-foliage migration path for tourists. When you reach the junction, you'll be in Williamstown, the site of the pretty Williams College campus. A drive along Main Street through the campus shows off its smooth green lawns and ivied brick buildings.

The college's art museum, the **Sterling and Francine Clark Art Institute,** holds one of the finest collections of nineteenth-century French paintings in the country. Among the more recognizable are those by Renoir, Mary Cassatt, Degas, Monet, and Berthe Morisot, hung in light and airy galleries that are a pleasure to stroll. Besides the French paintings, the museum also has eighteenth-century English silver, prints and drawings, and American furniture, silver, and paintings.

The museum is located ¼ mile south from the intersection

of Routes 2 and 7 in downtown Williamstown. It's open from 10:00 A.M. to 5:00 P.M. Tuesday through Sunday. Call (413) 458–9545 for information.

In and around the campus a number of restaurants have sprung up, several of them aimed at the pocketbooks of parents. But along Spring Street are a handful of inexpensive cafes designed for student budgets. One is the Cafe at the College Bookstore, at 76 Spring Street (413–458–3350), a bookstore-cafe open only in summer. Seating is mainly on an outdoor terrace, where lunches of sandwiches and open-face melts are served, along with cappuccino and espresso. A few doors down, at 27 Spring Street, is the Cobble Cafe (413–458–5930), a funky place whose light fixtures are paint buckets and colanders. It serves breakfast and lunch, and lunches include lots of veggie and pasta dishes and such items as chicken curry crepes and cold sesame noodles.

At the **Western Gateway Heritage State Park** (413–663–6312) in North Adams, the railroad history of North Adams comes alive in a thoroughly entertaining way. Housed in six old wooden railroad buildings, the park also includes a cluster of shops and restaurants, linked by a cobblestone courtyard and black iron street lamps.

The visitor center tells the story of the building of the 4¾-mile Hoosac Tunnel through 2,500-foot-high Mount Hoosac—one of the greatest engineering feats of the nineteenth century. The project claimed the lives of almost 200 men and took twenty-four years to build. The ring of pickaxes, the shouts of men, and the dripping of water can be heard inside an old boxcar through an imaginative audiovisual presentation. Here in the eerie darkness, you experience the same working conditions the tunnelers did. The tunnel made North Adams "the western gateway" to commercial travel from the East, a long-sought goal. North Adams also became an important railroad town. Children can ride a miniature train around the freight yard in good weather.

The park is well marked by signs off Route 8. It's open daily from 9:00 A.M. to 8:00 P.M. from the first Sunday in May through the first Sunday in November. In winter, the park closes at 4:30 P.M., except Thursday, when it's open until 8:00 P.M.

In a spot in North Adams, glacial melt rushing over limestone deposits carved out a deep chasm and left an arch above it, the only "natural bridge" in North America. Now the centerpiece of a state park, the **Natural Bridge** is made entirely of marble. A walkway high and narrow like a catwalk lets you peer over and around the Natural Bridge from almost any angle. Chain-link fence ruins the photo opportunity; on the other hand, it keeps people from falling in and killing themselves. Despite the mighty forces that shaped it, the Natural Bridge itself is quite small—a span of some 20 feet—and so dark inside that it looks cavelike. Still, something about it mesmerizes. A few picnic tables spread about a grassy area in earshot of the water are a nice spot to lunch.

The park is open from 10:00 A.M. to 6:00 P.M. weekdays and until 8:00 P.M. weekends and holidays, May 15 to October 30. Call (413) 663–6312 or (413) 663–6392 for information.

Heading down Route 8 into North Adams, you'll pass right by two tasty places. The first is The Big Dipper, at 24 Marshall Street (413–663–9411), which reputedly has the best sandwiches in town and the best homemade ice-cream in the Berkshires. It still retains the feeling of the 1930s lunch counter and variety store that it once was. Serving breakfast and lunch, it offers overstuffed sandwiches, homemade soups and salads, and a wide variety of its famous ice creams.

Undaunted by the cola giants, **Squeeze Beverages** of North Adams has been making its own brand of sodas since 1920, one of only a handful of independent bottlers left in New England. The twenty-eight flavors include sarsaparilla, birch beer, watermelon, and cherry cola, all sold in glass bottles. Because the glass bottles are so hard to come by, sometimes Squeeze has to make do with bottles carrying mongrel logos. Its own logo is cute: two children hugging on a park bench, encircled by hearts. There's a retail store in back of the factory outlet, at 190 Howland Avenue (Route 8); if you call ahead (413–743–1410), you'll be welcome to watch the bottling. The store is open 10:00 A.M. to 5:00 P.M. Mondays, from 9:00 A.M. to 5:00 P.M. Tuesday through Friday, and from 9:00 A.M. to 3:30 P.M. Saturdays.

Just east of North Adams, a few miles past the junction of Route 8, Route 2 takes a giant bend, almost 180 degrees. The loop-de-loop in the road practically derails buses and gives cars plenty of pause. It's called the Hairpin Turn, and it's an inspiring place to stop. It just happens to be situated at one of the most fabulous vantage points for viewing the Hoosac Valley. You're up so high here that it looks as though you could hang glide right down into the valley. Few houses mar the pretty bowl of greenery below, and the blue sky and clouds reach up in front of you forever. In the elbow of the turn, there's a small parking lot with observation telescopes set up for a closer look, behind which are a nondescript restaurant and souvenir stand.

As you come back down Route 8 into the center of Adams, just past the McKinley Statue on Park Street you'll see the Miss Adams Diner on the left. This is an original diner built in 1949 by the Worcester Lunch Car Company and has been nicely restored, with a green-and-white tiled floor, plenty of chrome, and the original Worcester Diner clock. The food is traditional diner fare.

As a last stop in the northern Berkshires, an unusual political footnote awaits in the town of Cheshire. Back in 1802, a local pastor decided that a nice gift for President Jefferson would be a cheese made by Cheshire farmers. A big one. Molding it in a cider press, the farmers made a 1,235-pound cheese—one day's product of the town's dairies. The cheese was drawn by oxen to Albany and was then shipped by water to Washington, D.C., where, on January 1, 1802, it was presented to the president with great fanfare.

In commemoration of this moment of glory, the Cheshire Cheese Press Monument stands on a corner, a concrete replica of the cider press used to make the cheese. To see the monument, heading south on Route 8, turn left onto Church Street, at the First Baptist Church. The monument is on the corner of Church and School streets, just opposite the Cheshire Post Office. Slow down or you'll miss it; it's not very big, and it could be partly hidden by children climbing on it.

Index

Index

About the Author

Patricia Mandell is a native New England freelance writer who has been specializing in travel writing for five years. She is a co-author of *Hidden New England* and *Hidden Boston and Cape Cod.* Her travel articles have appeared in many publications, including *Caribbean Travel and Life, The Walking Magazine, The Yankee Traveler,* the *Washington Post,* the *Miami Herald,* the *Kansas City Star,* and the *Denver Post.* She is a contributing editor of *Americana,* and a member of the Travel Journalists Guild and the American Society of Journalists and Authors. Ms. Mandell has also been a high-tech and business writer, and an editor for daily newspapers.

She researched this book while pregnant, hiking up to the Ice Glen and down to Bash Bish Falls, traversing the Glacial Potholes, and eating egg creams and chèvre. The writing, well, that she squeezed in in between the howling demands of her newborn daughter. Ms. Mandell lives on Boston's South Shore with her husband Eliot Lees and daughter Alexandra.